Problem Solving
the Creative Side of Mathematics

Derek Holton

The Mathematical Association

Supporting Mathematics in Education

Published by:

The Mathematical Association
259 London Road
Leicester LE2 3BE
United Kingdom

Telephone:

$$(44)\ (0)\ 116\ \ 221 \begin{cases} \text{Book sales} & 0014 \\ \text{Membership} & 0013 \\ \text{Fax} & 2835 \end{cases}$$

Email:

$$\begin{cases} \textbf{\textit{Book sales}} & \text{sales@m - a.org.uk} \\ \textbf{\textit{Membership}} & \text{office@m - a.org.uk} \end{cases}$$

Web:

www.m-a.org.uk

© **Derek Holton,** 2010

ISBN: 978-0-906588-71-0

Designed, typeset and illustrated: Mathscounts, London

Printed and bound in Great Britain: Blissett Digital Books, London
W3 8DH

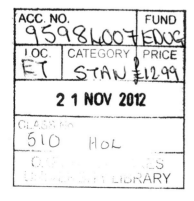

Dedication

I would like to dedicate this book to my wife Marilyn for all her help in all of life.

Acknowledgement

I would like to thank Leanne, Lenette and Irene (it is with great sadness that I realise that Irene will never see this book) for their secretarial support during the writing of this book and the articles that preceded it. I couldn't have done it without you.

I would also like to express my very sincere thanks for all the work that an unknown reviewer did for the vast improvement of the final product. Not only did they find every punctuation error, corrected some of the mathematics, and give valuable advice on presentation, but that person also gave me several nice mathematical ideas that have been included at various places in the text. I am extremely grateful for the reviewer's efforts. I would also like to thank the Editor, Barry Lewis, for all his work on making the finished book what it is. It has been a very positive experience working with him and I am very pleased with the results of that collaboration. Having said that, of course, the errors that remain in the text are the result of my own hand.

Introduction

This little book has grown out of the series of twenty articles that appeared under the heading "Holton on Problem Solving" in the *Mathematics in Schools* journal published by the Mathematical Association of Great Britain. The aims of that series were to provide a variety of problems that teachers could use with students who have a range of ages and abilities and to show how those problems might be developed further. They were virtually all tried and true problems that I had used myself with students in primary school and secondary school and with teachers at workshops and conferences.

As I developed the problems I wanted to show teachers the side of mathematics that I had experienced as a mathematics researcher. This is a side that is completely different from the mathematics I had experienced at school myself and at least a little different from the mathematics that I have lectured to students at first year university. It actually wasn't until I was doing my Masters degree that I realised that there was more to the subject than learning a whole collection of algorithms and regurgitating them on demand. I suddenly discovered the creative side of the subject, what a Finnish colleague of mine, Juha Oikkonen, calls the '**human**' side of mathematics.

The point is that mathematics isn't just 'there' to be picked up and used. And what is 'there' didn't get 'there' by accident – well not totally by accident anyway. It got 'there' by lots of people spending untold hours thinking about it, struggling with it, talking to others about it and occasionally having that wonderful feeling of 'getting' it. Suddenly seeing all the pieces fit together is an exhilarating experience. I fancy that when Pythagoras 'got' his theorem (or whoever it was that 'got' it for him) he felt much the same elation as Picasso when he invented Cubism or Wagner when he put the finishing touches to *Der Ring des Nibelungen*.

And now for the commercial: you can feel that feeling too! What I, and many other mathematicians have discovered independently is that students solving mathematical problems not only go through very similar steps to mathematicians doing research, but they can also get the same pleasure out of it. I saw this again just recently when doing a problem solving session at a local girls' school. When one of them suddenly saw how the process we had been working on split the numbers up to 99 into three well defined groups, see Chapter 2, she exclaimed "**Wow!**".

So my real aim in the problem solving series and my real aim here is to open up this creative side of mathematics. I want people to see how interesting, puzzling and exciting mathematics is. I want them to see that solving a mathematical problem is like solving a murder mystery; it's like holding your breath for a long time and suddenly letting it out.

What's more I think that there are many more students who can appreciate this side of the subject and be active in it than we give them credit for. Not for the first time in the girls' class I was talking about earlier, I was reminded that you can't tell who the 'good' students are. Let me tell you about a girl I'll call Mary. Mary had been sitting through the session that produced the 'wow' with a blank look on her face. I knew that I had lost her. I tried a couple of times to bring her into the discussions without any success. So I moved on to the numbers up to 999. The girl next to Mary put up her hand and said "I can do all of that. Well, actually I can't, but Mary can." I asked Mary to write it on the board. Without any comment or even a smile she put up one piece of algebra and two columns of numbers. She had blown the extension to 999 apart. When I told her that that was brilliant, she betrayed a small smile on the edge of her lips, but only a small smile.

I also think that this approach to our subject will encourage students to put in a greater effort to master the fundamentals. Recently, in another school, I was trying to take students through an algebraic-like arithmetic argument. They were stumped. With the help of the teacher we worked through their difficulty with that mathematical argument that they had never seen before. They pretty well all slaved (I don't think that is too strong a word) away at the argument until when I extended the problem at least three of the students immediately were able to use the argument they had just learnt and most of the others got there before too long.

After the commercial comes the Health Warning. At this point I should say that this is not a text book in the normal meaning of the word. It is not written in the normal sort of mathematical way. Though you will find algorithms, theorems and proofs the journey to them is more important than getting them. (I can't believe I wrote that.) Above all, what I am trying to do here is to present a number of problems that might be useful and interesting, and show **how to go about solving them.** This means that I will come up with a lot of ideas for solutions not all of which will work. It also means that I will flit from one idea to another, even one problem to another. What I am trying to mirror is the problem solving process and this is anything but linear. I hope that it doesn't distract from your enjoyment and that you don't find it too frustrating.

This book is not a sanitised version of mathematical creativity. It's not the warts and all version either, but it does aim to show more of the action than is usual with mathematics books.

The way that I write will also mean that I give up on some problems because at the time of writing I didn't know how to solve them. I just have to leave things in the air. I don't know everything. I will never know everything. There is always going to be a question I can't answer. That's just the way it is.

I believe that that is exactly the same with teachers. Surely they don't know everything that there is to know even about a course they have given for years? Students must occasionally come up with a question or a comment or an idea that they hadn't thought of before. There is nothing wrong with this. It's just the way it is.

So don't be surprised when I quote a transcript of a lesson in which a teacher doesn't know something. The point that I am making is not that the teacher has a problem. I don't see anything wrong with the teacher not knowing this particular thing. At that point of the book I am just noting that scaffolding can be done by a student.

In the problem series of articles I mentioned above, I wasn't able to say and do all I wanted to. I haven't been able to do all I wanted to here either, but what I have done is to take some of the problems from that series and extended them a bit and talked a little more about their solution and about approaches to problems generally.

Let me say at this point that I have not included any mathematical modelling in this book. Nowhere do I look at a 'real world' problem and consider modelling it as an applied mathematician would. The reasons for this omission are partly that I know less about modelling than I do about problem solving and partly because after I said what I wanted to say about problem solving I didn't have room for modelling. That must await another book.

I hope through this book that you enjoy getting to see the Creative Side of Mathematics more clearly.

How To Use This Book

This is only advice, of course, but I see several ways to use this book for at least two types of reader: the problem solver and the teacher.

For you, the reader, every reader, I first have to explain the layout of the book. I move forward, most of the time, in fits and starts. These segmentations are signalled by what I call a **chevron**. It looks like this:

Think of it as the play button you might use when you have temporarily halted the action.

My intent here is that when you reach this icon, you will stop and do some work. Oh yes, I'm sorry, but to get anything out of life you have to put something in. To get anything out of this book you'll have to work at least a little. I once read somewhere, but I forget where "**The one who does the thinking does the learning**". I hope you will learn from this book so I guess I need you to think and to think means to work.

After a chevron, I often go down a completely different trail. You may find this annoying but it's my signal that it's work time. If you want to keep going on the first problem that you are working on, then you can skip to the next occurrence (or two), of a chevron where I almost certainly get back to the original idea again.

I recognize that this is a crazy way to go about things, but the chevrons frequently represent staging posts of the problem concerned. At each one you move just another fraction deeper into the problem.

If you are a problem solver whose main aim in reading this book is to solve problems, then you should start at Appendix I with any problem that interests you and work on it till you get as far as you can. Then go to the main text and see how your work compares with what I have written. Hopefully I have introduced some ideas that push your solution a little further. With any luck you will have done things differently from me and I'd love to see what you have done. Please get in touch - use email: **derek.holton@bigpond.com**

If you are a teacher, then I recommend that you first read the book as a problem solver and see where I finally take the problem. This often goes over two chapters as I have tended to take the article from *Mathematics In School* to start off with and then developed things further. This second chapter is usually where the proofs are.

Teachers should then go to Appendix II before introducing a problem to their class. This is where the staging posts are. They will suggest how you might tackle the problem with your class. Think about each of your students and where they might get with the problem because some students will get further than others. Plan how to move a given student from one staging post to the next.

I think that it is important for teachers to know as complete a solution of a problem as possible along with generalisations, in order to give worthwhile scaffolding. I have tried working with students on problems that I don't know how to solve completely. This has some benefits such as showing students what I do when I am working on an unknown problem. They like to think they are working on the unknown too. However, I'm not sure in these situations how best to scaffold them. Overall, I think that students will get a lot more from a problem if they are eased towards a solution.

I have to add a caution here. There is a fine line between moving students to a solution that you know and moving them away from a solution of their own. I well remember trying to push a group of three students once on to a solution I knew. Surprisingly they dug in their toes and they did come up with, for me, a new solution. But don't let students drift on a false trail for too long. Ah, but then, how long is too long? And how do you know it's a false trail?

Happy working.

1   *The 400 Problem*

A few years ago I went into a classroom very badly prepared. (I could make excuses.) Anyway, I had this problem that I'd found. I'll call it the '400 Problem'. Essentially, you have these two subtractions:

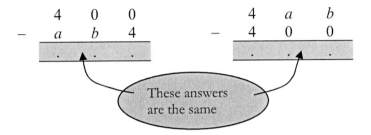

If you know the answers are the same for both subtractions, what are the values of *a* and *b*?

Now I had at least worked this one out ahead of time. I'd used algebra and I expected that the problem would keep the class busy for a while, while I gathered my wits. After all, they were a junior secondary school class and probably hadn't done much algebra. I thought that I could think what to do next while the class worked away.

It would be good if you could try the problem before I (we) move on.

▷   I had hardly written the problem on the board; I certainly hadn't had time to size up the class or to wander too far looking over students' shoulders to check their progress before up went a girl's hand. I went over to her expecting to be asked to explain what I meant by *a* and *b*. Instead she said "*a* = 3 and *b* = 6". I was flabbergasted. "How did you do that?", I blurted out, probably in an accusing tone.

"Well I did this, this, and that has to equal that, and it came out to *a* = 3 and *b* = 6." Not a smidgeon of algebra in the whole perfect argument!

On my side of the exchange panic was developing. How was I going to occupy the class for the rest of the hour? And then I had what was for me a brilliant idea. In my professional life extending and generalising is what it's all about. So I said, "What happens if you change all of the 4s to 5s?" And the problem had suddenly, inevitably, turned into mathematics. She was happy. I was happy too. Clearly I had time to think now because I knew that I had at least seven more problems up my sleeve. It didn't occur to me to ask her to check that her answer was right. Is it really true that 400 – 364 = 436 – 400? It's always worth checking though.

So what does happen if you change 4 to 5 everywhere?

   On reflection, I was a little surprised it hadn't taken the bright student at least a little time to understand the problem. Many students since have wanted to be sure that each time they saw an '*a*' it stood for the same number; and the same for the '*b*'. And surely it takes a little while to think how you might tackle the problem. Is there some nice systematic approach or do you just have to use trial and error, or better, trial and improve? No, this girl had gone straight to the point. Not bad really as she had a better solution than I did.

What about you?

Suppose that we **did** use trial and error. What if we 'trialled' *a* as 5 and *b* as 1? Then we'd have

$$
\begin{array}{ccc}
4 & 0 & 0 \\
- \quad 5 & 1 & 4 \\
\hline
\cdot & \cdot & \cdot
\end{array}
\qquad\qquad
\begin{array}{ccc}
4 & 5 & 1 \\
- \quad 4 & 0 & 0 \\
\hline
\cdot & \cdot & \cdot
\end{array}
$$

Obviously, the sum on the left has a negative answer (–114) while the one on the right gives 51. As they aren't the same we didn't guess right. On the other hand, that guess has told us that *a* must be less than 4 (is that clearly true?). Why don't we improve our guess to *a* = 1 and *b* = 5?

$$
\begin{array}{ccc}
4 & 0 & 0 \\
- \quad 1 & 5 & 4 \\
\hline
\cdot & \cdot & \cdot
\end{array}
\qquad\qquad
\begin{array}{ccc}
4 & 1 & 5 \\
- \quad 4 & 0 & 0 \\
\hline
\cdot & \cdot & \cdot
\end{array}
$$

Now the left and right sums still don't have the same answer but we can see that, by increasing *a*, we can get the two answers closer together. Surely, if we then fiddle with *b*, we'll get the right answer in just a few more iterations.

▷ But let's look at what the young student had actually done. Maybe you have done it that way too. It doesn't take algebra. Even primary students can (and have done since) solve this problem. She simply said something like, "From the left subtraction, 4 from 0 you can't do, so borrow 1. Then 4 from 10 is 6. In the subtraction on the right, 0 from *b* is *b*. But the two subtractions have the same answer, so *b* = 6."

"In the left subtraction, 6 from 9 (she changed the 0 to 9 when she borrowed the 1) is 3. On the right side, 0 from *a* is *a* and that must be 3. "So, *a* = 3 and *b* = 6."

▷ But right now I should say that, at some stage, this problem or its solution (and the problems and solutions that are going to follow in this book) are going to stretch your mind and, eventually maybe, stretch it too far. All the problems I'll be talking about have various levels. So if you are reading this book for fun, don't be afraid to break off at any point. Also know that if you are reading it in the hope that you might find something useful for your class, then most of the problems in this book suit a range of students and they can be stopped at whatever level suits your class or any given individuals in the class. You can find more details on staging points in Chapter 6 and Appendix II.

▷ Anyway, not long after the girl had produced her correct answer, hands were popping up all over the place. Mostly they were right and I asked them to change all the 4s to 5s, and later 4s to 6s, and so on.

About here I brought all the class together so that no one was left too far behind. I asked the girl to tell us all how she got her answer. I checked to see if anyone had used another method. There was not an algebraic solution in sight! But there was another approach that might have evolved from the trial and error approach above. That said:

"From the right sum, the answer has to be less than 100. So from the left *a* has to be 3. It's also clear that *b* = 6."

	4	0	0			4	3	*b*
−	3	*b*	4		−	4	0	0
	.	3	?			.	3	?

I'm always wary about "clear" in a mathematical argument, but I guess that you can find b by some more trial and error if necessary. After all, the right sum answer has to be the two-digit number ab and now we know that a = 3. This gives an answer of 3b for the left subtraction. So what b from 0 (on the left) will give you that 3? If it's not 6 then it can only be 7 surely. But it's easy to see that that isn't any good. Maybe it **is** clear that b = 6.

We talked about the two solutions. Now that everyone in the class had a method they could use I sent them back to change 4 to 5 to 6 … Actually, I divided up the class into four groups and got them to do two each from 1, 2, 3, 5, 6, 7, 8, 9.

While the class was slaving away I wrote this table on the board. Here the n was the 4 that I started with or the numbers that we replaced the 4s by.

n	1	2	3	4	5	6	7	8	9
a				3					
b				6					

As students completed a value, I got them to fill in the appropriate place on the table. Other, slower, students checked the value when they had completed the calculation. There were a couple of errors, but we quickly sorted them out.

Then, miraculously, and this was more than I deserved, there was a pattern. So we all looked at that for a while to see what we could see. Actually it's amazing that different people could see different things, but one interpretation was that

$$10a + b = 9n.$$

Actually they said "ab = n" but I changed the ab to 10a + b because I didn't want them to be confused between ab as a **two-digit number** and ab as the **product** of a and b.

Another interpretation of the pattern was

$$a = n - 1 \text{ and } b = 10 - n.$$

Yet another interpretation of the pattern is

$$a + b = 9$$

but, of course, these last two are related. All of this may be seen from the completed table.

n	1	2	3	4	5	6	7	8	9
a	0	1	2	3	4	5	6	7	8
b	9	8	7	6	5	4	3	2	1

So I told them about theorems – these are just true statements. And that mathematicians, especially pure mathematicians, just love to find theorems. I'm not sure now if they had heard about Pythagoras' Theorem. That's probably the only theorem that most adults seem to have heard of though, despite the fact that every mathematician for ages has been trying to accumulate theorems to help to understand their world (and maybe ours too).

I also told the students how we had just proved a theorem. We'd done it the hard way. We had checked every case. Now that's not a fancy way to prove a theorem, but it's what just came to us and it worked, so accept it – you don't get to prove a theorem every day. The theorem said that if we had the two subtractions below

$$
\begin{array}{cccc}
 & n & 0 & 0 \\
- & a & b & n \\
\hline
 & . & . & . \\
\end{array}
\qquad\qquad
\begin{array}{cccc}
 & n & a & b \\
- & n & 0 & 0 \\
\hline
 & . & . & . \\
\end{array}
$$

and both subtractions gave the same answer, a and b had to be the values, in terms of n, in one of the boxes above.

Actually the method we used in the proof is sometimes called **Proof By Exhaustion**. This is not because it had exhausted us, though maybe it had exhausted one or two of the students, but rather that we had exhausted every possible case so the result had to be true. We had covered all nine possible values for n in the table above, so we had proved the result.

▷   But the bell hadn't rung yet in the class I was working with and it wouldn't do so for a little while. What to do now? Extend the problem again! Surely that's what any good mathematician would do? Such a person would want to push this 400 Problem as far as she possibly could. So now I decided to try the **4000 Problem**.

Assume that I had *a, b* and *c* that had fixed values and suppose that I had two subtraction sums like this.

```
      4   0   0   0                  4   a   b   c
  –   a   b   c   4              –   4   0   0   0
     _____           _____
      .   .   .   .                  .   .   .   .
```

If those two subtractions are equal, what values do *a, b* and *c* have?

Everyone set off with great enthusiasm. But no girl put her hand up. Neither did any boy. Actually a strained atmosphere beset the room. Some children were talking to each other in puzzlement. Then someone put up a hand and made a suggestion, but it wasn't a confident suggestion.

"$a = 6$, $b = 3$, and $c = 6$. But that doesn't seem right."

"Why not?"

"It makes the left subtraction negative."

If you apply the girl's method of the 400 Problem to the 4000 Problem, you surely get those values and they don't work!

We had come across a situation that couldn't be solved. There was no answer to this problem. I had invented a problem that couldn't be solved! Have you heard of any maths problem that doesn't have a solution? It's like the mathematical equivalent of the English language problem of being able to say something that you can't write down. Yes, you can actually say something in English that you can't type in Word! For example, the farmer was out in the field sowing his crop. His wife was in the farmhouse sewing his socks. In fact they were both ~~sowing, sewing~~, ...!

We talked about this impossibility of the 4000 Problem for a while. You can actually prove that the problem is impossible by using a **Proof By Contradiction** but let's not worry about this now. Gödel was the man when it came to things impossible; see

http://en.wikipedia.org/wiki/Kurt_G%C3%B6del

Roughly speaking he was able to prove in 1931 that there were true statements regarding things as simple as numbers, that can't be proved from the axioms on which they are based. You can imagine that this was a bombshell of nuclear proportions at the time and it completely upset the mathematical apple cart of the 1930s - not to mix my metaphors you understand.

Anyway, we weren't involved in anything quite as deep as Gödel's Incompleteness Theorem and we then decided that it might be worth trying the **40000 Problem** just in case it was solvable. The class, though, was equally divided between those who thought it might work and those who thought it wouldn't.

What do you think? What do you get?

 The best thing to do here again is to try an example. If it works, it works and if it doesn't, ... er ... it doesn't.

$$\begin{array}{ccccc} 4 & 0 & 0 & 0 & 0 \\ - \quad a & b & c & d & 4 \\ \hline \end{array} \qquad \begin{array}{ccccc} 4 & a & b & c & d \\ - \quad 4 & 0 & 0 & 0 & 0 \\ \hline \end{array}$$

So:

- Taking the girl's approach, we can't take 4 from 0 on the left but we can take 4 from 10 if we write the 4000 that's there now as 3999. So 4 from 10 is 6. By looking on the right we see that that makes $d = 6$.

- Back to the left, d (= 6) from 9 gives 3. Looking to the right gives $c = 3$. Does that bring back memories?

- Back to the left, c (= 3) from 9 gives 6. Looking to the right gives $b = 6$.

- Back to the left, b (= 6) from 9 gives 3. Looking to the right gives $a = 3$.

We get a repeating 3, 6, 3, 6 pattern. And exactly the same sort of thing happens if we change the 4s to 5s or any other digit. With 5s instead of 4s we get $a = 4$, $b = 5$, $c = 4$, $d = 5$. I'm sure that you can get the rest for yourself. We essentially get the same answer as we got in the n00 case, but we get things repeating. Armed with that breakthrough, you might want to conjecture (guess) what happens for the n00000 and the n000000 and the n0000000 Problems. And are you going to prove these by exhaustion? And if you do, would you want to prove the

*n*00000000000000000000000 Problem

that way? After all there are only 9 values that need to be considered for *n* so how bad could that be?

What would you do?

> But I didn't show you my approach to the 400 Problem. If you want to skip this algebraic approach on your first read through I will totally understand. First of all I made the Problem into an equation with each side of the equation standing for one of the subtraction sums. That gave me

$$400 - ab4 = 4ab - 400$$

However, that wasn't much use until I expanded the *ab* bits. You see *ab*4 is really

$$a \times 100 + b \times 10 + 4$$

while 4*ab* is really

$$400 + a \times 10 + b.$$

Armed with that extra piece of information I got

$$400 - (a \times 100 + b \times 10 + 4) = 400 + a \times 10 + b - 400.$$

This gives

$$396 - (100a + 10b + 4) = 10a + b,$$

and

$$396 = 100a + 10a + 10b + b.$$

And that simplifies to

$$396 = 11(10a + b),$$

or

$$36 = 10a + b$$

From that you can read off *a* = 3 and *b* = 6.

That argument has a certain amount of sophistication. Having seen that, you can probably understand why I was totally non-plussed when the young lady came up with her answer in no time flat.

But if that method works for the 400 Problem, why doesn't it work for the 4000 Problem? Let's put the equation together and see where things go wrong.

$4000 - (a \times 1000 + b \times 100 + c \times 10 + 4)$
$$= 4000 + a \times 100 + b \times 10 + c - 4000.$$

With a little bit of algebra you can get this down to

$$3996 = 11(100a + 10b + c)$$

And that reveals a problem. The fact is that 3996 **isn't divisible** by 11! And it would have to be for this equation to hold because the expression in brackets in the last equation has to be a whole number.

So there's another proof that the 4000 Problem can't be solved. You don't need a Proof by Contradiction, after all. So what do you think of the chances of the 400000 Problem having a solution? I expect an answer to this before you move on.

$\triangleright$ While I don't recommend inventing problems on the run like that even though it worked for me that particular time, I hope some of the adults and children who have encountered this activity at various levels have enjoyed it and experienced something of the way mathematicians go about their work. This problem really does contain experimenting, conjecturing, proving, extending and generalising. All these are the mathematician's tools of the trade and I'll have more to say about them later (Chapter 3).

But I can't resist one final extension in this chapter. Perhaps you would like to think about just one last problem. What answers would you get to the 400 Problem if I told you that everything that we had been talking about was in base 8 and not in base 10? Would you be able to show, for example, that in the **400 Problem base 8**, you would get

$$8a + b = 7n$$

And how did I get that anyway? And could that be generalised for all bases?

2   *Other Subtraction Problems*

In the previous chapter we completely solved the 400 Problem
and hinted where you might take this further. Towards the end of this
chapter we'll completely solve the $40 \cdots 0$ Problem (for all positive
numbers of zeros and, of course, with all 4s replaced by your
favourite digit *n*). However, first it appears that there are a number
of subtraction problems around so let's have a look at a couple of
them here and try to see how far we can go with them.

> **The Difference Problem** Take a two-digit number *ab*.
> se
>   the order of the digits to get *ba*. Subtract the smaller of these
>   from the larger. Repeat with the result and keep going until
you find something interesting. How's that for an ill-defined
problem? Let me help you out by doing one or two examples to get
you started.

Let's take 73 as an example.

73	63	72	54	90	81
−37 →	−36 →	−27 →	−45 →	− 9 →	−18
36	27	45	9	81	63

I'll stop there because I've been to 63 − 36 already.

What happens with 51?

51	63	72	54	90	81
−15 →	−36 →	−27 →	−45 →	− 9 →	−18
36	27	45	9	81	63

Oh! That's a bit surprising! 51 and 73 both behave in the same way.
Is that an accident?

I'll leave it to you to figure that one out. Try a few more examples. (By the way it is not a capital offence to use a calculator or even program a computer! Either of these will considerably speed things up for you here. They are also likely to be more convincing than your own hand calculations.) Hopefully something interesting comes up pretty quickly. Look for a conjecture or a pattern, or extend or generalise what you have found. Is there a theorem or two hidden in there somewhere regarding two-digit numbers?

 A 1089 Problem Here's the second of the two problems I promised you. Look at this

> I've called this 'A 1089 Problem' because there are other problems where the number 1089 features.

	321	198
First this	−123 →	+ 891
	198	1089

	724	297
and then this	−427 →	+ 792
	297	1089

If I take any other three-digit number *abc*; reverse its digits to get *cba*; subtract the smaller from the larger to get *pqr*; reverse its digits to get *rqp*; and add *pqr* to *rqp*, deep breath, will I always get 1089? And if I do, why do I?

What I'm saying is, does the following always work?

$$
\begin{array}{r}
abc \\
- \underline{cba} \\
pqr
\end{array}
\quad \longrightarrow \quad
\begin{array}{r}
pqr \\
+ \underline{rqp} \\
1089
\end{array}
$$

I'd like to have the number **1089** in flashing, questioning, lights but the publisher won't let me go that far – some fussing about cost I think.

Do you always get 1089? Well obviously not. No it's not obvious perhaps until you have done a lot of examples and maybe accidentally come across something that didn't give you 1089. Accidentally doing things reminds me of the psychology experiment I heard about when I was doing my teacher training. The researchers had set up a lever so that when a cat patted the lever with its paw it was rewarded with food. Unfortunately on the first day of the experiment one particular cat accidentally knocked the lever with its rear end as it walked by. Food appeared. Forever after this, the cat fed itself by hitting the bar with the aft section of its anatomy …

But perhaps you don't need an accident. Perhaps you found one or two examples for yourself. Possibly you don't need an accident to tell you that if the number *abc* is **palindromic** then

A **palindrome** is a number that reads the same backwards and frontwards - something like 353 or 747 or, even longer, 123454321.

$$abc - cba = 0$$
and $$0 + 0 = 0.$$
You might like to see:

http://en.wikipedia.org/wiki/Palindromic_number

Since the course of true mathematics doesn't run smooth, it's likely that there are difficulties with other *abc* numbers. But if you do find some problems think how to overcome them and just keep on going anyway with as many numbers as you can.

Where did you get on the Difference Problem? Did you find that most numbers got stuck in cycles? All except palindromes of course and they immediately went to zero.

Let's forget about palindromes for a moment or two. What have you found while you've been experimenting with lots of two-digit numbers? Do all other numbers seem to come to rest in that 5-cycle of numbers that I found when I did the calculations for 73 and 51 a little while ago. Given that the two-digit numbers sort of hunt in pairs, I'll write the cycle as five pairs of numbers (63, 36), (72, 27), and so on.

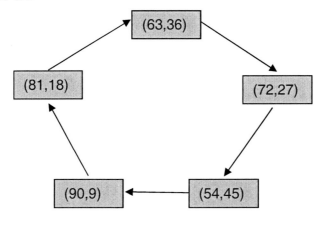

All the numbers in this 5-cycle are multiples of 9. Are all the multiples of 9 there? The ones less than 100 anyway. Since $12 \times 9 = 108 > 100$, we only have to worry about the first 11 multiples of 9. There are 10 in the cycle … Hey! One's missing! 99. Why isn't 99 on the cycle?

There are a couple of reasons for this. First of all 99 is a palindrome and I said to forget about them. Of course, I can't be sure that 99 heard me. On the other hand, how would you get 99 by subtracting one two-digit number from another? 99 − 0 might do it but in the Difference Problem we have to reverse a number somewhere. So how can $ab - ba = 99$? No way! If ab is a palindrome, then $ab - ba = 0$. If ab isn't a palindrome, then ab is already less than 99. So 99 can't come up on our cycle. It can only be listed among the palindromes.

Ah! Now I can begin to see that all two-digit numbers (I guess we have to allow some one-digit ones too because 09 has appeared on the cycle but I'll treat all one-digit numbers n as $0n$ so that I can reverse them to get a two-digit number) can be put in a little group together because of this problem. If a number is a palindrome then it is in a group by itself. This group goes straight to zero on reversing and subtracting. Then there are the ten numbers (five pairs) that are non-palindromic multiples of nine. They go round the cycle as we reverse and subtract. So where do all of the other numbers sit? At least in a group around the cycle? But where exactly?

So far we have four numbers that hop straight onto the cycle. 73 and 51 and their reverses 37 and 15, all do that. Can we show that **all** the non-palindromes immediately go into our cycle? Or can we find some numbers that keep to themselves, either for a while or for ever?

When you think about it, no two-digit number can do anything **forever** that's different. After all, if you do operate on a given number more than a 100 times you **have** to come back to a number that you have already come across. So all numbers have to close up in some way. At the moment we only have two choices for this behaviour: either they go to zero (like the palindromes) or they go into a 5-cycle. The question now is, are these the only two possible behaviours? Could some number you haven't tested yet go to the cycle after one or two iterations of the process? Or is there some other, completely different cycle, that we haven't found yet? That's worth a little thinking about. I'll come back to that later.

▷ The last time we were looking at the 1089 Problem we had this difficulty about whether all non-palindromic numbers behaved properly or not. Did you ever come across anything like 524? Look at this.

$$
\begin{array}{r}
524 \\
- \,425 \\
\hline
99
\end{array}
$$

The question is, can 99 equal *pqr*? Actually if I break tradition and write 99 as 099, then *rqp* = 990. What's more 990 + 099 = 1089. So maybe convention tells us that if we get a two-digit number *pqr* after subtracting *cba* from *abc*, then we should think of *p* as being 0. We've already had to do something like this for the Difference Problem so it's not a great leap to do this now. Remember, a few moments ago when we made 9 an honorary two-digit number? I hope that difficulty didn't worry you too much.

I'm assuming then that you overcame any little difficulty like this that you met and have by now churned out a large number of examples. Apart from the palindromes, you should always have found that you got 1089. How can we solve the 1089 Problem then? Presumably as a result of your work and my work we can make a reasonable conjecture. But, before we do, we need to say precisely what the process is that we are using, in order to make the statement of the conjecture precise.

So we'll say this.

> We get the **grunt** of a 3-digit number *abc* when:
> * we subtract the smaller of *abc* and *cba* from the other to get *pqr*
> * and we then add *pqr* to *rqp*.

Along the way we note that *p* might be 0 and *p* and *q* might both be zero. So now for the conjecture.

> **Conjecture**   The grunt of a 3-digit palindrome is zero and the grunt of any other 3-digit number is 1089.

Do you agree with that? If you don't, then make up and prove your own conjecture.

Now how to solve it? Well I don't suggest that you try Proof by Exhaustion on 999 three-digit numbers. Well, half of that number because if you do *abc* then you'll have done *cba* too. And you don't need to consider one-digit or two-digit numbers. OK so it's less than 500 but it's still too large to do every single case. Unless you have access to a technological device that you can program, it will take far too long to do it this way and this time you certainly will be exhausted by the time you've finished it all. You **have** to find a general approach.

I think it might be useful to try to analyse a particular three-digit number's grunt to see how we might treat the general case. I'll use 482 and use the same sort of method that I used in the last chapter with the 400 Problem.

$$
\begin{array}{ccc}
482 & & 198 \\
-284 & \longrightarrow & +\,891 \\
\hline
198 & & 1089 \\
\end{array}
$$

$$482 = 4 \times 100 + 8 \times 10 + 2$$
$$284 = 2 \times 100 + 8 \times 10 + 4$$

So what is really going on here?

$$
\begin{aligned}
482 - 284 &= (4 - 2) \times 100 + (8 - 8) \times 10 + (2 - 4) \\
&= (4 - 2)\,[100 - 1] \\
&= (4 - 2) \times 99 \\
&= 2 \times 99.
\end{aligned}
$$

Hmmm! That's interesting. Do we get that factor of 99 no matter what values of *a, b* and *c* we take? We certainly did with our two examples 321 and 724. In their cases we had $198 = 2 \times 99$ and $297 = 3 \times 99$, respectively. What's more the 2 in the factor of 198 is the difference between 3 and 1 in 321 in the same way that it was the difference between the 4 and the 2 in 482. What's more for 724, *pqr* has a factor of 3, which is exactly the difference between the 7 and the 4!

Is *qpr* always a multiple of 99 too? If so, what multiple of 99? And is 1089 a multiple of 99 - yes, it's 11 × 99! Is it true that *pqr* = ($a - c$) × 99 and *qpr* = [11 − ($a - c$)] × 99? It would be neat if that happened. That's all very interesting but can we do something like that without actually working it all out because we've got to be able to handle **all** three-digit numbers? I'm afraid that here's where I have to do some more algebra.

$$abc - cba = (a \times 100 + b \times 10 + c) - (c \times 100 + b \times 10 + a).$$

If we tidy this up a bit we get
$$abc - cba = (a \times 100 - a) + (b \times 10 - b \times 10) + (c - c \times 100)$$
$$= 99a - 99c$$
$$= 99(a - c).$$

Just what we wanted, but how do you manage to show that
$$qpr = [11 - (a - c)] \times 99 ?$$

It turns out that you don't have to do that by algebra. A little Proof by Exhaustion will do, given that there are only a few cases to deal with.

▷ But our Difference Problem will benefit by a little algebra too. Actually it's the same as we've just done, only easier. Recall we were trying to see what happened to two-digit numbers, *ab*, when we reversed and subtracted. We'll look at this, or at the very least, look at the answer to this!
$$ab - ba = 10a + b - 10b - a = 9(a - b).$$

Every difference ends up as a multiple of 9, even if *ab* starts off as a palindrome! So every number either goes to zero (if it's a palindrome) or it goes on to the cycle (if it isn't already there). So we don't have numbers rambling haphazardly all over the place. There are just three types of number and they are all well behaved. Roll on the drums, a theorem comes.

Theorem: in the difference Problem there are only three types of numbers
  Type I: the palindromes that go to zero;
 Type II: the ten numbers on the cycle that just
         cycle around for ever;
 Type III: all other numbers that go straight to
         the cycle.

I leave you to complete the proof.

Now I don't want to be push my luck here, but can we tell whereabouts on the cycle a Type III number hits? Experiment!

 Did you manage to find out how
$$pqr = 99(a - c)$$
leads to $qpr = [11 - (a - c)] \times 99?$

Think about it. How many multiples of 99 are there? Clearly just 10:
$1 \times 99 = 99$; $2 \times 99 = 198$; $3 \times 99 = 297$; $4 \times 99 = 396$;
$5 \times 99 = 495$; $6 \times 99 = 594$; $7 \times 99 = 693$; $8 \times 99 = 792$;
$9 \times 99 = 891$; and $10 \times 99 = 990$. First of all, like the 99 in the Difference Problem we can't get the 990 here. So forget it.

Then look at $2 \times 99 = 198$. Reverse 198 and you get 891. And 981 $= 9 \times 99$. But 9 and 2 are 11 so we've done that one. But if you do that with all the others (and there are only four more to do so it's not much effort) you'll find that reversing you get the '11 minus' factor of 99 that you want. Bingo!

But I know that you think that that is messy and I know that you really would like to see my algebraic proof of the 1089 Problem that has nothing to do with multiples of 99. Well here it is.

Let's start with an example to make it easier to follow. What I am trying to do here is to make the difference an expression in 100s, 10s and units. That way I can find out what *p*, *q* and *r* are so that I can reverse the digits to get *rqp*. So I'll start with the difference expression I had earlier in the first line and then massage it a bit in the second line. Then the third line should follow easily.
$$482 - 284 = (4 - 2) \times 100 + (8 - 8) \times 10 + (2 - 4)$$
$$= (4 - 2 - 1) \times 100 + 100 - 10 + [10 + (2 - 4)]$$
$$= (4 - 2 - 1) \times 100 + 9 \times 10 + [10 + (2 - 4)]$$

How about that? So here, $p = 4 - 2 - 1$, $q = 9$ and $r = 10 + 2 - 4$. Surely this will work for any non-palindrome number! Just change 4 to *a*, 8 to *b* and 2 to *c*. Then you get
$$pqr = (a - c - 1) \times 100 + 9 \times 10 + [10 + (c - a)]$$

So $pqr + rqp = \{(a - c - 1) \times 100 + 9 \times 10 + [10 + (c - a)]\}$
$$+ \{[10 + (c - a) \times 100 + 9 \times 10 + (a - c - 1)\}$$
$$= (10 - 1) \times 100 + 18 \times 10 + (10 - 1)$$
$$= 900 + 180 + 9$$
$$= 1089 !$$

Ah well!

So now to the complete picture of the Difference Problem for two-digit numbers. It's all in the factor of $a - b$. We know that

$$ab - ba = 9(a - b),$$

so the multiple of 9 that you hit first, if you are a Type III number is given by $a - b$. It takes the values shown in this diagram:

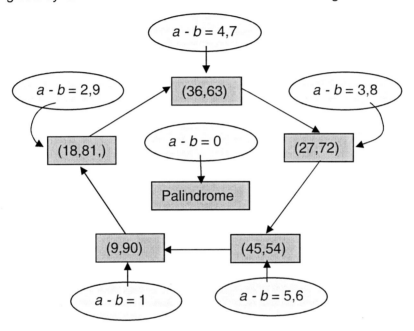

There is just one more wrinkle; I notice we can't enter the five-cycle at 90, but this is because we can't get $a - b = 10$!

Now that whole process should tempt you to attack the three-digit version of the Difference Problem. We know from what we did from the grunt problem that $abc - cba$ is a multiple of 99. So we might hope that all three-digit numbers hit some cycle at one of the multiples of 99. But in the two-digit case we had five pairs of numbers in the five-cycle. Will there be five pairs of numbers in the three-digit case? How might they be paired? In the two-digit case did you notice that the pairs of $a - b$ numbers in the diagram added up to 11 (except when $a - b = 1$). And we know that if

$$pqr = 99t \text{ then } rqp = 99(11 - t).$$

So that's probably it.

Is the figure below the final answer? (I stopped to do some calculations while you weren't looking.) What Types of numbers exist here?

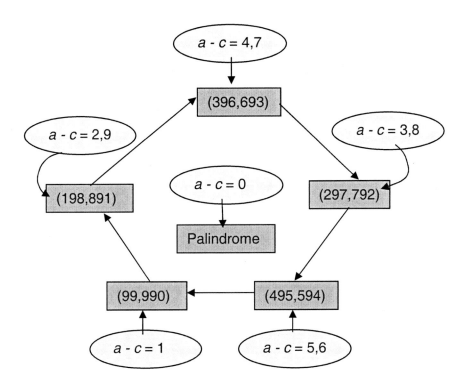

Does that mean that this continues to go on and on for four-digit and five-digit and *d*-digit numbers?

I'm afraid that life, mathematical life anyway, isn't that easy. What actually goes on in the four-digit case?

 And a wet Sunday in front of the fire might be dedicated to looking at seeing what happens to the grunt of four-digit numbers. Except who has fires these days?

But I'll do one to whet your appetite.

$$
\begin{array}{r}
5712 \\
-\ 2175 \\
\hline
3537
\end{array}
\quad\longrightarrow\quad
\begin{array}{r}
7353 \\
+\ 3537 \\
\hline
10890
\end{array}
$$

That's scary! Apart from the palindromes is the grunt of every four-digit number 10890?

On mature, later reflection, it became clear what was going on in the generalisation of the 400 Problem so I wrote it up, in algebra! To start with, I've gone back to the previous chapter and have started to have a look at the 40000 and above Problem. First of all, I can write

$$\overbrace{4000\cdots000}^{r\ \text{zeros}}$$

where there are r zeros as 4×10^r. So if you look at the 4×10^r Problem, it seems that you will always get a solution if r is even and you never get a solution if r is odd. For r even the answer is $a = 3$, $b = 6$, $c = 3$, $d = 6$ $e = 3$, $\cdots$, and so on.

When you think about it, there is no way you can prove this by exhaustion. There's no way you'll live long enough to do all of the cases. But this is where the power of algebra comes in. So my original approach had some merit after all.

Doing this in its fullest generality, we're trying to solve the $n \times 10^r$ Problem.

	n	0	...	0	0		n	a	b	...	u
$-$	a	b	...	u	n	$-$	n	0	0	...	0

So $n \times 10^r - (ab \cdots u0) - n = n \times 10^r + (ab \cdots u) - n \times 10^r$.

That's going to be nicer if we let $ab \cdots u = m$, because this gives

$$n \times 10^r - 10m - n = n \times 10^r + m - n \times 10^r.$$

Tidying up we get
$$n(10^r - 1) = 11m.$$

Now it's a fact that you probably know, but can easily check (or even prove), that 11 divides $10^r - 1$ if and only if r is even. Hence we know when to expect a solution and when a solution won't exist. But it's also true that when $10^r - 1$ is divisible by 11, the answer is $9090 \cdots 0$ with $r - 1$ digits. So

$$\boxed{m = 9090 \cdots 9n}$$

and we can read off the values of the digits of *m* directly from this. You can also do this whole thing by **Mathematical Induction**, but

      (i) I haven't told you what that is yet,

and

      (ii) maybe it's too much to expect a simpler proof than this algebraic one anyway. I use the word 'simpler' here in a relative sense.

 Just in case you think that mathematics will ever come to an end have a look at this.

Take any four-digit number whose digits are not all the same. I'll choose 8012. Now put the digits in descending order to get 8210. Next reverse the digits, 0128. And, of course, now subtract the smaller from the larger, to give 8082. Because this is so much fun, do it all again with 8082 and then with whatever number comes next, and so on. This gives us

$$
\begin{array}{ccc}
8820 & 8532 & 7641 \\
-0288 & -2358 & -1467 \\
\hline
8532 & 6174 & 6174
\end{array}
$$

It looks as if we are stuck with 6174 repeating endlessly. Try another starting point, 2375 say.

$$
\begin{array}{ccccc}
7532 & 7551 & 9954 & 5553 & 9981 \\
-2357 & -1557 & -4599 & -3555 & -1899 \\
\hline
5175 & 5994 & 5355 & 1998 & 8082
\end{array}
$$

which is what we started the last example with. So 2357 is driven towards 6174 as well. What you find is that **all** four-digit numbers (with at least two different digits) end at 6174.

This unlikely number is known as **Kaprekar's constant,** after the first person to discover this behaviour. Now Kaprekar's full name is Dattaraya Ramchandra Kaprekar, and he was an Indian schoolteacher/mathematician who lived from 1905 to 1986. So it is still possible for non-professional mathematicians to discover new things in mathematics. You just have to look in the right place with the right attitude.

The question is, what is the nice proof here? How can you prove that every four-digit number (with at least two different digits, we want to at least get rid of palindromes again) ends up at 6174 in the way described above? Well as far as I can find out there is no nice proof. You just have to do a proof by exhaustion. Not that you need to go through every four-digit number. You know enough now to realise that you can cut down considerably the numbers that need to be looked at, but even so there is no neat method that can be used here.

But, naturally, there are still questions to be asked. For example, what happens with 2-, 3-, 5-, 6- and n-digit numbers? Do they all have their own Kaprekar's constant?

I won't bother you with Kaprekar numbers, self numbers or even Harshad numbers right now as you have more than enough to be getting on with.

3 *What's This All About ?*

I think that there are times when you should jump straight into things. That's what happened in the first two chapters of this book. There was no introduction to explain what a problem is or how you solve problems, we just started. Of course, along the way there were some hints and suggestions, and, hopefully, you had enough background and native ability to make some progress. I hope you made a lot of progress but, if you didn't, you had some idea of what was going on.

I've sort of adopted more the approach of a first language learner than a second, although language by immersion is a credible technique. If you like, we've been learning problem-solving by immersion. In the process, a lot of new language and possible ideas arose without too much comment. In this chapter I want to bring language and action together to say what I think we have been doing up to now, what we'll do for the rest of the book and what that has got to do with mathematics.

I'll start us off with a diagram that, I hope, gives a good overall picture of what has been happening so far. It'll need explanation, of course, but that will follow.

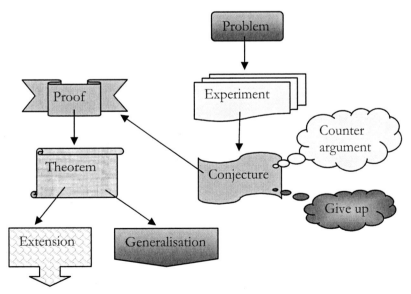

Figure 3.1 A model of an approach to mathematical investigation.

Problem

In the first two chapters we've essentially looked at four problems. These have been the 400 Problem, the Difference Problem, A 1089 Problem, and Kaprekar's Problem. By a **problem**, then, I mean a question that you don't immediately know how to solve, but that can be approached mathematically and a solution obtained. I deliberately said "a problem that **you** ⋯" because what is a problem for you may not necessarily be a problem for other people and vice versa. So some people may know immediately what to do and others will work out a plan of attack and still others will need help. I talk more about help in Chapter 6.

It turns out that many problems, like the four I mentioned above, can lead onto a great deal of mathematics, but no mathematics can start without a problem. Somebody at least has to say "I wonder if ⋯" before there is a problem.

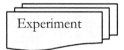
Experiment

One of the tools that we have already found useful for solving problems is **experimentation**. This is just one form of mathematical play. An experiment involves looking at something and seeing what you can get out of it – just trying to do something and hoping that it will lead somewhere.

In the 400 Problem we experimented at one point with trial and error. We put in some numbers for *a* and *b* and saw what we got. In the next two problems we just tried number after number in the hope that we would see a pattern. Where did all that lead?

The whole point of this experimentation is to extend our experience and, of course, some of it is actually fun. Why do children play? For the same reasons. Why do adults play? OK, maybe it's just to win but, surely, not all adults play solely to win.

And why do animals play? I've watched cormorants jumping off cliffs in high winds, gliding in a great arc back to the cliff, and then jumping off again. Of course, I don't really know if they are doing it for fun, but it **looks** fun. And it's hard to see why else they would be doing it. Of course, it's probably valuable flying experience that stands them in good stead when they are caught in bad weather out fishing, but are they consciously thinking "I'll just jump off here so that I'm a better flyer"?

Mathematicians also engage in some sort of play, mathematical play, as they press on to find theorems.

 Our main reason in experimenting in mathematics is to look for patterns so that we can make **conjectures**. These are just guesses, but guesses backed up by experiments and our past experience. They are guesses not as to what the patterns are, but what we'd like them to be. The problem is that in practice a mathematician's strike rate on conjectures is pretty low. Conjectures are, however, a very good mechanism to make progress to the final result. They help expand experience and they help to narrow in on the actual, 'true', situation.

One conjecture you might like to make, because it follows on from the earlier cases, is that 4-digit numbers in the Difference Problem all end up on a five-cycle made up of multiples of 999. That is clearly false because 7887 goes 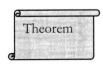 straight to 0 as it's a palindrome. So the presence of 7887 provides a **counterexample** (or counter argument) to the conjecture.

So let's tidy up that last conjecture. To begin with, try: Any 4-digit number that is not a palindrome ends up on a five-cycle made up of multiples of 999?

That's OK until you find the counterexample of 5735. See what happens to this. How does the conjecture need to be refined now?

So if we make a conjecture we can keep testing it and, if necessary, make changes to it. This process leads us along a path that hopefully will lead to a **proof**.

 A proof is a mathematical argument that shows that nothing else is possible. The conjecture that we'd had up to that stage now takes on the rank of a **theorem**. This is a true statement for which a proof exists.

You remember that our first theorem was for the *n*00 problem and said that

$$\text{Theorem} \quad 10a + b = 9n.$$

Actually that result is really not big enough or important enough to be called a theorem. Maybe we should just call it a **lemma**, a sort of 'little' theorem. But never mind the name, it has a proof, and that's the key thing for mathematicians.

 You would not have failed to notice the part of the diagram that says '**give up**'. There are two reasons for giving up. The first is a temporary impediment, like a need for sleep – that can be forgiven. You can't do mathematics non-stop because some problems (most problems that are worth solving) take more than 10 minutes to solve. So you need to give up sometimes for a while.

Actually, giving up temporarily is a good problem-solving strategy. When you think you have stopped work your brain often doesn't. I think that I have a person in the basement of my brain. Often when I stop working on a problem that person doesn't. And every now and then, that person writes a brilliant idea on a piece of card and moves the card to the top part of my brain where I can read it. (You will realise that my brain has not yet come into the technological age.)

This sort of thing tends to happen after a period of intense work followed by rest. These are the ideas you get in the shower or, in the case of Archimedes, in the bath. These are the **Eureka experiences**. Actually other famous mathematicians have had them. Poincaré was coming home and had just stepped onto a bus when his brain-basement-person checked in. The idea was apparently so clear that Poincaré didn't even write it down. I must say that when I get an idea I write it down straight away. I have so few really good ones that I can't risk losing them!

Hamilton seems to have had my problem. He was strolling by the canal with his wife when he got his message about a problem that had involved him in lengthy thought. He was less restrained than Poincaré. He got out his pocketknife and carved the result on a bridge. I guess if he forgot it when he got home he could always nip back for a quick look. I'm sure that he wasn't really a vandal – he probably just hadn't got a pen and paper with him.

So giving up for now is OK. However, if you want your Eureka Experience you will have had to do a lot of hard work beforehand. The basement person isn't in to giving free gifts of good ideas. And then there is giving up forever. I only condone this action if you really have tried hard without success for several years or if you have died!

But a mathematician's work is never done. If a conjecture is rebutted by a counter argument, then it's back to experimenting and fishing for another conjecture. Even finding a proof doesn't warrant a rest. Then the mathematician has to move onto an extension or a generalisation and generally reflect on where he or she is mathematically.

In an **extension** you take the problem that you've been working with and alter it a little. The new problem is related to the original problem but doesn't contain it. So the 500 Problem, for example, is an extension of the 400 Problem; the Difference Problem for 3-digits is an extension of the Difference Problem for 2-digits. In these new problems you are just pushing out into unknown territory, changing something here and there to see what happens.

On the other hand a **generalisation** is a variation of the problem that includes the original problem as a special case. The  main example we've had here so far has been the $n \times 10^r$ Problem. This contains the 400 Problem as a special case. If you put $n = 4$ and $r = 2$ you get that special case. Putting $r = 3$ gets you the $n \times 1000$ Problem (which we know has no solution).

Generalisations are really what mathematicians are after. They want to be able to encompass as much into one theorem as they possibly can, so they chase after generalisations all the time.

And extensions are ways of moving mathematics forward into related areas. Of course, I'd like you to think that. In practice it often turns out that we can't prove the conjecture we'd like to, but we can prove something close to it. So we extend the original problem and prove the extension instead. Mathematicians aren't above a little cheating when it comes to getting new results.

Now the point of telling you all this is that this is the way pure mathematicians work. You need to know that they guess a lot and play a lot and generally enjoy themselves. They especially enjoy themselves when they find a nice example or guess a pretty conjecture or prove an elegant conjecture. They can be very unhappy if they can't find any one of these things for months!

And most of us don't enjoy 'writing up'. When we have a theorem or two we write up the results as a paper and send it off to a journal. Hopefully the referee there will accept the paper as being interesting and valuable, and the journal will publish it. That's especially good for our egos and it doesn't hurt academic promotion either.

I said the point of telling you this was that it is the way we work. But it is the way most people work on mathematical problems. Indeed it is probably close to the process that anyone, working on any problem, mathematical or otherwise, goes through. It's possible that Picasso went through a similar process on the way to cubism and Darwin on the way to evolution. In these more general settings the 'proof' aspect is slightly different from the mathematical one but it exists there just the same. But I suspect that there is something in common in the creative process no matter who is being creative with what.

Even primary students go through similar, recognizable, stages, when solving maths problems. I hope … No! I expect that you will too. You're certainly going to get my encouragement. In fact this whole book is just about getting to grips with this creative process. There are lots of problems and it would be good if you can solve some of them. But the real purpose here is to understand, to get comfortable with, and to be able to use the process encapsulated in **Figure 3.1**.

4   *The Six Circle Problem*

I've used the Six Circle Problem a lot because it shows how mathematicians tackle and extend problems. So here it is again.

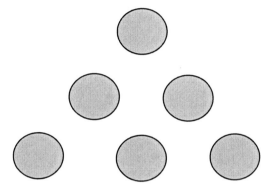

Figure 4.1 The six circle arrangement.

Is it possible to put the numbers 1, 2, 3, 4, 5, 6, one per circle, so that the three numbers on each side of the equilateral triangle above have the same sum? If so, how many ways can this be done? If not, why not? Extend or generalise.

What would you need to do if you were faced with this problem and there was no one around to help you? How would you tackle it?

I frequently find myself in this situation with the cryptic crossword. My wife and I try to have a restful hour or so every Sunday morning when she reads a book and I do the crossword. But it not infrequently happens that I look through all the clues and can't solve one of them. This is, of course, disastrous. I could mutter words that I can't write here, but I've set aside a restful hour for this ······ crossword and what am I going to tell my wife if I can't even get started?

There are strategies that then come into play, of course. Every cryptic crossword has a few anagrams. They are generally easy to pick out so that keeps me occupied for the next little while. Hopefully that gets me started. If I'm lucky too, I can usually spot words that end in "ING", for example. Now that may not help that particular word, but it may give me a crucial letter (I, N or G) in a crossing word. Generally, in this or similar ways I manage to pass away the hour profitably, even if it doesn't always mean complete success.

▷ So what can we do with the Six Circle Problem? Well, we can always guess, as indeed we did with the 400 Problem, earlier. Throw in some numbers and see what we get. Here are a few random guesses:

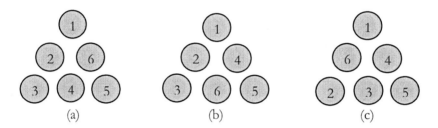

(a)   (b)   (c)

Figure 4.2 Some random guesses at solutions for the Six Circle Problem.

Unfortunately none of these work, but hopefully in the process we've come to understand what the basic conditions of the problem are. We know that we have to use the numbers from 1 to 6 once and only once, and the sums of the three numbers on each side of the triangle have to be the same. Clearly in (a), (b) and (c) they're not the same, but we've found two, (a) and (c), where **two** sides have the same sum, and one, (b), where all three are different. Not that that's any use to us of course! But we did come **very** close with (c).

We might also realise that any guess will give us five others because of the symmetries of rotation and reflection that an equilateral triangle has. For instance, if we rotated (a) clockwise we'd get a 1 in the right hand bottom corner, a 5 in the left hand bottom corner, and a 3 in the top corner but all the side sums would have been preserved.

Anyway, despite the fact that we haven't got an answer to the problem by this experimentation, we have at least managed to get a better idea of the problem and what it is asking.

▷ Can we be more **systematic** in our guessing? One thing I find is that even undergraduates are not good at being systematic. That's a pity because it's a skill that's valuable in a lot of mathematics and even in a lot of life.

What could we do here? Well, put 1 in the top circle and then 2, 3, … round the triangle to 6. Check: does it work? No, that's (a) after all. So now do 1, 3, 2… around to 6. And keep going till we have tried all 120 possibilities. Then put 2 in the top circle and start all over again. (How could we do the 400 Problem this way? Would we **want** to do the 400 Problem this way? Would we really want to do any problem this way?)

That's all very tedious, but at the end we would have exhausted all possibilities (as we did under different, and less exhausting, circumstances for the 400 Problem). And we would have answered some of the questions at the start of the chapter.

So being systematic **will** work here, and in many other places, but it will often take seemingly forever to complete. Of course, if you have a computer handy that you can program it. But even that won't work if the situation you are in, not only seemingly goes forever, but does actually go forever – like the $n \times 10^r$ Problem.

If we're not making progress with being that systematic, what next?

At times like this we're going to have to take a punt. Let's suppose that there **are** solutions to find. This in itself is a guess. It cuts down the directions we need to search. But mathematicians are far too sophisticated to take guesses, so we call them **conjectures**. They're the lifeblood of mathematics. There's nothing like a good conjecture to keep a mathematician happy (or even a bad one for that matter – they are much better at those).

> **Conjecture**: There is at least one answer.

So what? Well if there is an answer, then there must be a sum that's common to all sides of the triangle. Let's call that the **sum** of the solution. This is likely to be a key property. What could we do if we knew the sum? Wouldn't it help us to be systematic? We could certainly cut down a lot of the unnecessary work we were thinking of doing a minute ago. What other questions can we ask about the sum:

- How big could the sum be?
- How small could it be?
- Could it be odd/even?
- Could the sum be 8?
- Could the sum be 14?

 Could the sum be 8? Play around and see if that's at all likely. Could it be 14? Is that possible? The 8 looks too small doesn't it? There's this 6 that we have to use. Many students see (or rather 'feel') this straight away, but are unable to give a satisfactory argument. One or two will come up with this brilliant explanation though:

" *First 6 has to be somewhere:*
      (i)   *the smallest sum we can have will then need the*
            smallest numbers along with the 6;
      (ii) *these smallest numbers are 1 and 2;*
      (iii) *so the smallest possible sum is 1 + 2 + 6 = 9.*"

So far then, we have only shown that there can't be a sum smaller than 9. However, we haven't shown yet that there is one of these things. Let's call it a **blah**! A blah is a way of putting all the numbers 1 to 6 in the six circles so that the sums on each side are the same. How can we show that there is a blah whose sum is 9?

 The simplest thing to do now is to try to be systematic again. How can we get three of the numbers 1 to 6 to add up to 9? And remember we can't use any number more than once.

Be systematic and start big – **with the 6**. We now need two numbers to make 3, so they can only be 1 and 2.

$$9 = 6 + 2 + 1.$$

Now assume 6 isn't used (after all, we've produced all of the possibilities with a 6 in); **so try 5**. Now we need two numbers to make 4. Systematically (starting big) we get two possibilities: 3 + 1 and 2 + 2. But we can't have 2 + 2 ! So

$$9 = 5 + 3 + 1.$$

OK, so now **try 4** and ignore 6 and 5. We have to make 5 with two numbers. Systematically, we have 4 + 1 and 3 + 2, and that's all. But we can't have 4 + 4 + 1. So

$$9 = 4 + 3 + 2.$$

Then we have to **try 3** as the biggest number. But that implies three 3s. So systematically we've found all the sums that are possible in this problem. There are only three. So we must be done. Why?

$$9 = \begin{cases} 6+2+1 \\ 5+3+1 \\ 4+3+2 \end{cases}$$

▷ We can't have a sum of 8. But what about 14? Think about the argument we've just used. Can we turn that around? We can and it should show us that there is no sum bigger than 12.

▷ The important thing now is, not only to look at what we've done, but also at where it leads us. It often takes students a while before the penny drops on the three numbers summing to 9. (What's the significance of the numbers that appear in more than one sum – the numbers in bold above? What can we do now?)

That's the Desert Island method of solution where I've assumed there's no one around to help. But in a classroom someone usually finds a solution and then someone else. And then, despite a lot of effort, no more seem to be forthcoming. At that stage it's a good time to make a conjecture.

Conjecture: There are precisely *S* answers (blahs) to the Six Circle Problem. (*S* maybe 1, 2, 3, or more. Put in whatever value you think *S* is.)

Can you prove this? How? Is there a counter argument? Here that means, 'Can someone find another answer?' Then the Conjecture moves up to *S* + 1. Can you prove this? How? Is there a counterexample? Can we use the method we did for the blah with sum of 9 to get all the rest? ...

- **And is there another way to solve this problem?**

Hopefully, by now, you've looked at the 1. It has to go somewhere and the largest side sum it will be involved in is if it is paired with 6 and 5. So the largest sum we can have is 12. All we have to do now is to repeat the work we did with the blah with sum 9, in checking each of the sums 10, 11 and 12. That has to lead us to a Theorem.

 Maybe at this point you're beginning to realise why problem-solving is so difficult. There are often so many things going on all at once.

Afzal Ahmed and his colleagues came up with the idea of a **rich mathematical problem** some time ago. See, for example,

http://www.iis.ac.uk/view person.asp?ID=13&type=auth

A rich problem is one that leads to lots of new ideas and directions, and can be solved in a lot of ways. The Six Circle Problem is one of those. The 400 Problem doesn't do too bad a job either.

I think about now we have proved the following result.

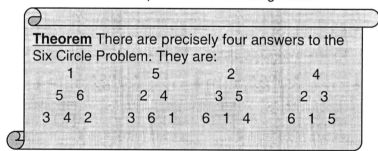

Theorem There are precisely four answers to the Six Circle Problem. They are:

1	5	2	4
5 6	2 4	3 5	2 3
3 4 2	3 6 1	6 1 4	6 1 5

Of course this is not a theorem until we have proved it, but we have the ammunition to do that. We can whittle the possible number of sums down to 9, 10, 11 and 12. Then we can show that each of these sums can only be made in three ways. Then we can put these ways together to form a blah. So we have a proof.

I'm sure that many of you will be disappointed that we haven't used algebra at all in this proof! It can be done though. I won't do it right now, but I might later on. But I wanted to point out that there **is** another method of proof of the theorem. The reason for that is to say that a lot of mathematics can be done in more than one way. In my research experience, after a group of us had proved something, we found another, often nicer proof, as we were writing the proof up for a journal.

Now look at each of the four blahs in the theorem and see what's going on in and between them. Then you might see how to reduce the length of the proof.

▷ Actually there are some interesting things going on in those four blahs that we have listed in the Theorem above. Suppose that you think of the numbers being written on a strip of rubber and the rubber placed over the circles. What happens if you move the rubber strip one circle round in a clockwise direction?

And what happens if you change every number on one of the blahs in the following way:

$$1 \leftrightarrow 6, \quad 2 \leftrightarrow 5, \quad \text{and} \quad 3 \leftrightarrow 4 ?$$

Does any of that save you some work in the proof of the Theorem?

▷ Let me point out again that if you don't do the proof you can't be certain you know the result. For now, I just want to emphasise that what we have as a Theorem would only be a Conjecture without the proof. Furthermore, proof is at the heart of mathematics and we shouldn't shy away from it. I think that we should encourage children to justify their mathematical statements right from their first day at school.

Mathematics is not mathematics without proof. If things aren't being ＿ ＿ a level that is understood, then it isn't ＿ upils in schools aren't being asked to prove or ＿ are doing, then they aren't doing mathematics.

＿ ull the Six Circle Problem apart a little because I ＿ we might have come to the point where we have to generalise the Problem:

＿ d we have six circles?

＿ id we have the numbers 1 to 6?

＿ lid we have an equilateral triangle?

＿ ve get anything interesting by varying one or all of ＿ ?

＿ ing the realm of extension and generalisation. But, of ＿ ve been here before. We did this with the 400 Problem. ＿ that we changed the 4s to 5s to 6s to 7s to ⋯ then we ＿ 00 to 4000 to 40000 to ⋯ Each of these individual steps ＿ **tension** of the original problem. They each produced a new problem very much like the original problem but slightly different from it. However, when we went from the 400 Problem to the *n*00 problem we produced a **generalisation**. We then had a problem that asked what happens for a number of values of *n*. If we put *n* = 4, we get back to the original problem; the 400 Problem is a special case of the *n*00 Problem; so the *n*00 Problem generalises the 400 Problem.

$$
\begin{array}{ccc}
4 & 0 & 0 \\
-\quad a & b & 4 \\
\hline
\cdot & \cdot & \cdot
\end{array}
\qquad
\begin{array}{ccc}
4 & a & b \\
-\quad 4 & 0 & 0 \\
\hline
\cdot & \cdot & \cdot
\end{array}
$$

$$
\begin{array}{ccc}
n & 0 & 0 \\
-\quad a & b & n \\
\hline
\cdot & \cdot & \cdot
\end{array}
\qquad
\begin{array}{ccc}
n & a & b \\
-\quad n & 0 & 0 \\
\hline
\cdot & \cdot & \cdot
\end{array}
$$

How can we extend or generalise the Six Circle Problem? There's more than one way to do this, but I'll look at the following generalisation.

> **A Six Circle Problem Generalisation:** What sets of six numbers are *nice*?

That is, what sets of six numbers can be inserted in the six circles so that the sum of the three numbers on each side is the same (they form a blah)?

Notice that I've introduced the definition of '**nice**' to avoid saying, each time, all that stuff about what the six numbers do. Mathematicians introduce definitions because they like to be precise and concise (or perhaps they are just lazy).

Now {1, 2, 3, 4, 5, 6} is surely nice. And if we had a condition for **any** nice set, then {1, 2, 3, 4, 5, 6} would have to satisfy it. It would be a special case of the big result, so the big result would indeed be a generalisation.

There are some obvious sets that are nice. Clearly, because we can use the original four arrangements as a basis for them,

- {2, 4, 6, 8, 10, 12},
- {9, 10, 11, 12, 13, 14}

- {5, 8, 11, 14, 17, 20}

are all nice sets. What's more they all produce four possible arrangements. There might be a nice conjecture for you here. Something about multiples of the numbers 1 to 6? No, you can go further than just multiples. It looks as if we might be able to take each number in turn, multiply it by some fixed number and add another fixed number. For instance,

$$5 = 2 + 3 \times 1 \qquad 8 = 2 + 3 \times 2 \qquad 11 = 2 + 3 \times 3$$

$$14 = 2 + 3 \times 4 \qquad 17 = 2 + 3 \times 5 \qquad 20 = 2 + 3 \times 6$$

If you change the 2s here to any other number you like, say 13, and the 3s to any other number you like, say 56, the resulting six numbers can still be shown to form a nice set. You just put the new numbers in the places where the 1, 2, 3, 4, 5, 6 were originally. Actually the fun here is to see how the sum of the blah changes when you do that. Can you predict what it's going to be ahead of time?

There is clearly an infinity of such sets. Suppose we say that these sets are **arithmetic sets**. I've suggested (and you can show) that arithmetic sets are nice. But the big question now is, are all nice sets arithmetic?

This takes me onto another important mathematical idea, that of equivalence, or necessary and sufficient conditions or if and only if. Having shown that statement A implies statement B, mathematicians dearly want to know if B implies A. If it does we say that A and B are **equivalent**. But why would you bother? Firstly it's a sense of neatness or balance or interest on mathematician's part. It would be nice if there was this two-way relation between the statements so it's worth finding out just for interest. But secondly it can be useful. Suppose you have something that you think might be an A. To test it out you have to check all of its conditions. But if A and B are equivalent, we could also check out our something with the statement B. And it may be easier for a number of reasons to check B than to check A. So proving equivalence can be very useful.

But let's get back to the arithmetic set idea. You may need to play around with that notion of arithmetic sets for a while, and you should, but, of course, I have to move on. I hope to come back to it though.

Extension to the Six Circle Problem: Is the set {1, 2, 3, 4, 5, 7} nice? If it is, how many blahs can you get out of it? If it isn't, why isn't it?

This, undoubtedly, requires some experimentation. When you've done that for a while, I'd expect you to come up with a conjecture or two. Then perhaps a proof might be in order.

Just because I can, I want to look at $T = \{1, 2, 3, 4, 5, 7\}$ through an algebraic lens, as they say. You don't have to do this and if you are a bit 'algebraiphobic' you might want to skip this. However, a quick skim through the algebra will have two possible advantages for you. First it might show you whether or not there is a blah here, and how many there are. Second it might show you how to get an algebraic proof of our Theorem, just in case that might be useful.

Anyway, let's be positive and assume that T is nice and that it has a sum of s. I've drawn T below without the circles.

$$a$$
$$b \qquad f$$
$$c \qquad d \qquad e$$

If the numbers of T line up as above,

$$a + b + c = s$$
$$c + d + e = s$$
$$e + f + a = s$$

So adding them all together,

$(a + b + c + d + e + f) + (a + c + e) = 3s.$

We can simplify this by noticing that

$$a + b + c + d + e + f = 1 + 2 + 3 + 4 + 5 + 7 = 22.$$

Now it maybe that $a \neq 1$, $b \neq 2$, etc., but the sum of the numbers in $\{a, b, c, d, e, f\}$ has to equal the sum of the numbers in T. This now gives us

$$22 + (a + c + e) = 3s.$$

OK, so a, c and e are numbers from T such that when you add them to 22 you get a multiple of 3. I guess we can find all of these by being systematic. After all, the smallest candidate for $a + c + e$ is $1 + 2 + 3 = 6$ and the largest is $4 + 5 + 7 = 16$ so there are not too many sums to pick through.

With some trial and error we get

$$22 + (1 + 2 + 5) = 30 = 3s \qquad \therefore \qquad s = 10.$$
$$22 + (1 + 3 + 7) = 33 = 3s \qquad \therefore \qquad s = 11.$$
$$22 + (2 + 5 + 7) = 36 = 3s \qquad \therefore \qquad s = 12.$$

So the possible side sums here are 10, 11 or 12. But this time 11 is a problem. You can't make 11 in three ways. You can only do it twice!

$$11 = 7 + 3 + 1$$
$$11 = 5 + 4 + 2.$$

But you can do 10 and 12 in three ways and they lead to the following blahs

```
      1                        4
    4   7                    5   1
  5   3   2                3   2   7
```

So T is nice; it is not an arithmetic set; and we only get two blahs. It looks like we've got counterexamples for two possible conjectures.

 But what is the general form of all nice sets?

$$a + b + c = s$$
$$c + d + e = s$$
$$e + f + g = s$$

By subtracting in pairs,

$$a - d = e - b = c - f,$$

can you get a generalisation from there?

If you really want to know what nice sets look like, you should now spend some time playing around with arbitrary sets of six numbers with a view to making up nice sets.

$$a$$
$$b \quad f$$
$$c \quad d \quad e$$

Let $a = 10$, $b = 6$ and $c = 24$. What values do the other three numbers have to have? You see that we are experimenting again. This time just put a few numbers in and see what numbers this forces. Does this give you an idea of a conjecture about nice numbers?

5   *The Three Circle Problem*

Put any numbers you like in the three circles below. Add the numbers on each of the three sides of the triangle, as in the example on the right.

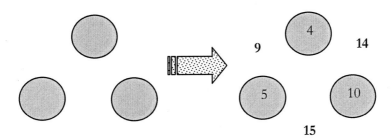

Figure 5.1   The three circle arrangement.

What interesting questions arise:

- what conjectures can you make?
- what conjectures can you prove?
- what extensions or generalisations can you dream up?

The emphasis I want to put on the mathematics now is on finding questions rather than solving them. So I'm going to take a simple situation, similar to the Six Circle Problem that we covered pretty fully in the previous chapter, and see what problems we can get out of it. Naturally I can't follow what you are doing, and a book has to have things written on the pages, so I'm going to go off on my own little trail. But that doesn't mean that my trail is the **right** and **only** trail. Don't take a peek ahead at what I've written. Sit down and try something out. Have a go. I'll still be here when you want to come back.

 So how did you go with the Three Circles? What have you seen? What have you conjectured? What have you proved? What have you generalised? Did you enjoy yourself?

I have no idea what you've done, but from here on I'll concentrate on three things relating to the side sums. These are when:

- all the side sums are equal;
- when the side sums are consecutive numbers;
- everything else. (Well, maybe not quite everything. Oh I don't know though.)

Let's concentrate on the first for a moment. Did you produce any examples where all the side sums were equal? If you did, what did you notice about those side sums? To get a better idea of what's going on here, let's try an example.

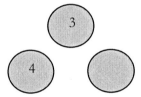

Figure 5.2 Two circles filled.

If I put 3 and 4 as shown I get a side sum of **7**. Now I can get a side sum of 7 on the right side by putting a 4 in the empty circle. And that's the **only** way I can get 7. That's of course a nuisance because I now get 8 as the bottom sum. But it does show me that 3 and a 4 was a bad choice. And I can now see that I won't get equal side sums unless I change the 4 to 3 (or the 3 to 4). The former change forces me to put a 3 in the remaining circle. So I'm sure that this approach will lead me to a justification that the only way to get equal side sums is to put the same number in each circle. That's rather boring, of course, though I can spice it up by noticing that if I put n in any circle I get equal side sums of $2n$. Which leads to two questions:

- is it possible to get equal side sums of 7?

and more generally,

- is it possible to get odd side sums?

Well, we all know about fractions. No one ever said that we should limit ourselves to whole numbers in the circles. So we can get equal side sums of 7 if we are prepared to put 3½ in each circle. Is that cheating? Why not allow *any* real number? I don't think that you should be prejudiced against fractions or decimals. Nor should you be prejudiced against π or e or any other irrational number.

 What can we say then about side sums that are consecutive? Did you get anything like that? I've put one in the diagram below.

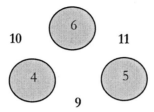

Figure 5.3 Consecutive side sums

Can (did?) you find any others? Are there any patterns here that are worth looking at? Can you justify those patterns? After a bit of effort you can probably see that taking any three consecutive numbers and putting them in the circles gives rise to consecutive side sums.

> **Theorem**: Numbers n, $n+1$, $n+2$ give rise to
> sums $2n+1$, $2n+2$, $2n+3$.

And, if you have to, you can justify this by using a little algebra. But do you have to use algebra to show this? Presumably not, but it does make it simpler to write down.

At this point you might begin to see that consecutive sums that are found by using whole numbers are restricted in some way too. What way? How can we get **all** strings of three consecutive numbers? Indeed, **can** we get all such strings?

But before I do that, if I'm given three consecutive numbers as side sums, is there a way of finding three numbers to put in the three circles to get these sums? Let's take 17, 18, 19, for example.

> **A Three Circle Problem Extension:** How can I find numbers to put in the three circles to produce side sums of 17, 18, 19?

I suppose that's not too hard if you've done a bit of algebra, but I want to use something else if possible. There's always guess and check. What if we guessed 5 in the top circle? Looking at the 17 and 18 gives us circle numbers of 12 and 13. But clearly 12 + 13 = 25 ≠ 19. Now, we could get another starting number other than 5 and keep going. That could get tedious if I asked for side sums of 2937, 2938 and 2939, though. There are a lot of possible guesses. Is there a way of using guess and improve? In other words, can we start with the failed 5, 12, 13 and push the guess to a better guess?

▷ A little while ago I noted that the consecutive numbers that we were finding tended to be restrictive in some way. If I stick to whole numbers in the circles, then my strings of three consecutive numbers always start (and end) with **odd** numbers. If I want to get 100, 101, 102 it's likely that I'll need to use fractions again. What are these fractions? Can you get them by algebra, by guess and improve, or is there some other method that you can use that I haven't even thought of yet?

I think after a little experimenting, given the side sums, you should be able to see that all you have to do is a bit of halving and rounding to go from consecutive side sums to circle entries. And if you want to allow for **any** string of three consecutive numbers you can, and, given the side sums, there are **unique** circle entries.

▷ Where do we go from here? Of course I haven't spent anytime on '*everything*' yet, but there's more to do before that. So what if we had 8, 10, 12 or 240, 243, 246 as our side sums? What circle entries would be needed in these two examples? Are the circle entries in these cases unique? So, can we generalise by allowing the consecutive number sequences obtained for the side sums to be any arithmetic progression? Does this force the circle entries to be in arithmetic progression? Are we limited to whole numbers or could we take the side sums to be 11.35, 18.35 and 25.35?

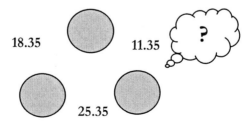

Figure 5.4 Non-integer side sums.

Let's try a bit of guessing and checking on that last example. What if I put 5 in the top circle? Then I'll get 6.35 and 13.35 in the other two circles. But 6.35 + 13.35 = 19.70 which is short of the 25.35. How short? 5.65. What happens if I distribute 5.65 equally between the 6.35 and the 13.35? Now 5.65 ÷ 2 = 2.825, and 6.35 + 2.825 = 9.175 and 13.35 + 2.825 = 16.175. (A quick check shows that 9.175 + 16.175 gives 25.35; so I've fixed that side sum.) Given bottom entries of 9.175 and 16.175, can I get right the top number? Is 11.35 − 9.175 the same as 18.35 − 16.175? Does that work? What's really going on here? Have I found a quicker method for finding circle entries, given side sums in arithmetic progression, than using algebra? Is there a quicker method still? But will this method prove that:

- we can get circle entries for any side sums in arithmetic progression;
- those circle entries are also in arithmetic progression; and
- the circle entries are unique, given the terms in the arithmetic progression?

▷ Back to the Three Circles for a final fling. It's time for that final ... **everything else**. (Well, maybe not quite everything ...) Presumably you can get any three numbers as side sums if you try hard enough. Take 94, 110 and 256, for example.

If I go about things as I did with the sides in arithmetic progression I would start with 5 in the top circle. When you think about it though, it would be much easier to put a zero there. At least it would then be easier to produce the two numbers that give side sums of 94 and 110!

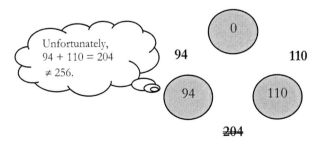

Figure 5.5 Everything else ··· maybe

Small swear words here. But 256 − 204 = 52, so why not add 26 to both 94 and 110?

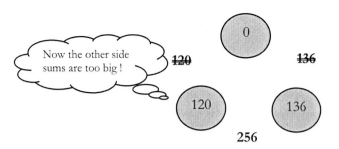

Figure 5.6   Everything else $\cdots$ not.

That leaves me the job of removing 26 from the zero. So the entries are now –26, 120 and 136:

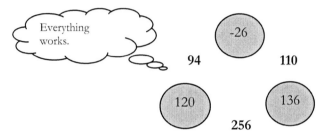

Figure 5.7   Everything else $\cdots$ solved.

Actually what I have invented here is an **algorithm**. That's a step-by-step method for getting the answer I am looking for. Once you know the steps you only have to apply them by rote (a computer could be programmed to do it) and you get the answer out.

Of course, that raises more questions than it settles:

- First there is the question of uniqueness. Are the numbers –26, 120, 136 the only circle entries that will produce side sums of 94, 110 and 256?
- Second, we need to ask if this process will work given any side sums?

Hmm. Until I've settled these two questions I really don't have an algorithm. Algorithms must work for all values and must give unique answers. But there are other problems to think about:

- Third, are the differences between the side sums the same as the differences between the circle entries?

- Fourth, if the answer to the last question is yes, how are the differences between side sums reflected in the circle entry differences in general? That is, where are they placed relative to each other? Where does the biggest number go in the circle given that the biggest sum is on the bottom side?
- Fifth, what happens if we restrict our circle entries to positive numbers?

Finally, for the moment, how can we prove any of these other than by algebra? On that last point, it's unlikely that doing a few more examples will get us there. There are most likely an infinite number of situations here and we can't settle all of these by a finite number of examples.

▷ While you're thinking about that, I'll start to move onward and upward. Since four comes after three let's move to four circles and the numbers 1, 2, 3, 4. This is sort of a 'back to the Six Circle Problem' and a downsizing. Are things more interesting for the arrangement of four circles in a square than they were for three circles in an equilateral triangle?

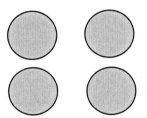

Figure 5.8 Four circles.

I guess that things are a little different here. After all we do get *three* different results (see below) just by putting 1, 2, 3, 4 in the circles. However, none of them have all side sums equal, though one of them does give four different side sums.

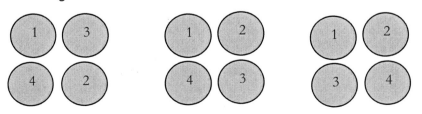

Figure 5.9 Using 1,2,3, and 4 in four circles.

We should probably discuss the case where all four side sums are equal. This is slightly more interesting than in the triangle case – we are not restricted to all the numbers being the same as we were in the triangle case. But it's still not absorbingly interesting.

What about the other problem then? If I gave you the four side sums (all different) could you tell me what numbers I'd have to put in the circles to achieve those sums? And would the inserted numbers have to be unique?

Are we about to get a general idea here? Take any n circles and arrange them in a regular n-sided polygon. Put the numbers 1 to n, one per circle. Can you show that no arrangement will produce n equal side sums? And can you show that we'll only get equal side sums if all of the inserted numbers were equal? On the other hand, if I were to give you n different side sums, could you tell me how to recover the numbers in the circles; that these numbers would be unique; and that you didn't need algebra to do it?

Please don't be guided too carefully by what I have said above. I've made at least one error. As a general rule you should not believe all I say. In fact you shouldn't believe anyone else either, especially a mathematician, until you are fully able to justify the result for yourself, or at least till everyone else has done the justification to your satisfaction. If you look back I've asked you to take some things in faith. Don't take things on faith!

 I'm about to take one of my usual swings in another direction. Until I started working on this chapter, it never occurred to me to work backwards on the original Six Circles set up.

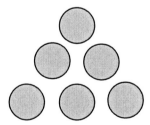

Figure 5.10 Six circles.

Can we find six numbers, one for each circle, that make up three *given* side sums? That might be too hard to begin with. So how about three *equal* side sums? And, a related question, if we only use whole numbers (all different!), what side sums can we make anyway? That ought to keep you going for hours in front of the TV with a pencil and paper. It might even rival the popularity of Sudoku. Well, perhaps not!

And certainly 'perhaps not'. It only took me a few minutes to realise that I could get a side sum of 3 by using all 1s as I have done here.

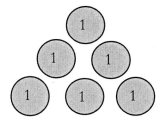

Figure 5.11 Sudoku ··· perhaps not.

And I can get any sum greater than 2 by changing two of the 1s to an appropriate *n*. The diagram below gives me a side sum of $n + 2$.

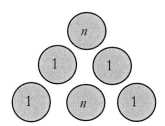

Figure 5.12 Side sum of $n + 2$.

(While we're on that, you can't get a side sum less than 3 if you are only going to use whole numbers.) But you might say that using 1 as many times as you like is cheating. Let's suppose then, that all the numbers have to be different. Ah, but that's not too much of a problem either. We already know how to get a side sum of 9. We can do that using the numbers 1 to 6.

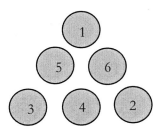

Figure 5.13 Side sum of 9.

Now repeat the same trick that we have just pulled. Change the 1 to $n + 1$ and the 4 to $4 + n$. Then we'll have side sums all equal to $n + 9$ for any n!

There is, of course, a small problem here for $n = 1, 2, 3, 4$ and 5. In those cases we get some of our digits repeating. But this can easily be avoided if we change 4, 5, 6 to $4 + n$, $5 + n$ and $6 + n$, respectively. Looks like you need something else to do while you're listening to your favourite music!

How about we think about how we would find the six numbers if we were given three *different* side sums? No, how about we don't because that's going to be harder to do than those configurations we started the chapter with. So let's go back to them and let me first confess my sin with the squares. Clearly, the side sums of squares with four circles can be equal without all of the inserted numbers being equal. And this is where n-sided polygons for n odd and n even differ.

 And that has to bring us back to the four circle case. Can I find the numbers to put into the four circles if I know the four different sums? Once again I'm bound to try an example.

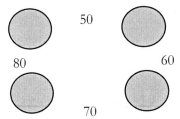

Figure 5.14 Four circles with given side sums.

Now it may come as a surprise to you to know that I can't do that problem – no matter what sorts of numbers I try. Why is that? Can you do it? Think about what is going on. The top left and the top right numbers add to 50. The top right and the bottom right add to 60. So the bottom right must be 10 more than the top left.

That's fine, but apply the same argument to the sums 70 and 80. That will show that the top left number is 10 more than the bottom right. That's clearly crazy! You can't find numbers to put in these circles!

Would it help if I changed the bottom side sum to 90, say?

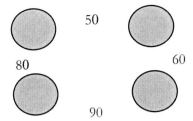

Figure 5.15   Four circles with a different bottom sum.

Now I have guessed that 10 (top left and going clockwise), 40, 20 and 70 will work and they do. But 20, 30, 30, 60 work too. And so do 100, –50, 110, –20! What's going on here? It looks as if I can take **any** number I like in the top left circle and then I can find a value for the rest of the circle numbers. These numbers aren't unique at all! This is totally different from the Three Circles case where I got unique answers. And in the Three Circles case every set of side sums seemed to produce a set of circle numbers.

There's something weird going on here. Maybe I should restore my confidence by doing a 5-gon problem. I have to say that I broke off here to check things out. Yep! That's fine. I didn't have any trouble with the examples I did there. In fact I didn't even need algebra! It seems to me that I can just extend the algorithm I used for 3-gons by one step to get an algorithm for 5-gons. Hey, and I bet I can make that work for 7-gons, 9-gons and any *n*-gon for *n* odd (and bigger than 3). But can I really do that?

 I left a couple of things to tidy up with the algorithm for finding the circle entries given the side sums. First of all what are the steps of the algorithm?

The Three Circles Algorithm:
Step 1. Put a zero in the top circle; put the left side sum in the bottom left circle; and put the right side sum in the right bottom circle.
Step 2. Add the bottom two numbers; subtract that number from the bottom side number; and add half the difference to the bottom two numbers;
Step 3. Subtract that half the difference from the top number.

I now have two things to do. First, I have to show that the algorithm gives me an answer no matter what the values of the original side sums are. Second, I have to show that the answer is unique. And I'm going to try to do that all without algebra. (If you are an algebra fan then now is the time for you to work it out that way.)

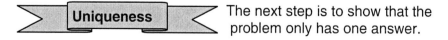 **Existence** Let's call the left side sum, 'left', the right side sum, 'right', and the bottom side sum, 'bottom'. So after Step 1 the circles contain 0 (top), left (left bottom), and right (right bottom).

At this point the sum of the bottom two numbers is left + right. Suppose we call the bottom sum minus this value, diff. Then add half of diff to left and right. So the bottom numbers are now: 'left + ½(diff)' on the left and 'right + ½(diff)' on the right.

Now subtract ½(diff) from 0 in the top circle.

At this stage we just have to add up the circle numbers to make sure that we get the original side sums.

left side: $-1/2(\text{diff}) + [\text{left} + 1/2(\text{diff})] = \text{left}.$

Good.

right side: $-1/2(\text{diff}) + [\text{right} + 1/2(\text{diff})] = \text{right}.$

Nice.

bottom side: $[\text{left} + 1/2(\text{diff})] + [\text{right} + ½(\text{diff})] = \text{left} + \text{right} + \text{diff}$
$$= \text{bottom}.$$

Brilliant!

So we have shown that the algorithm at least gives us one correct answer. Is there more than one correct answer?

Uniqueness The next step is to show that the problem only has one answer.

To do a uniqueness proof we have to first suppose that you can get two answers and then show that they are the same answer. So suppose that my two sets of circle answers are top, leftb, rightb; and Top, LeftB and RightB. Then the sum of top and leftb is the same as the sum of Top and LeftB; and the sum of leftb and rigthb is the same as the sum of LeftB and RightB. (This is because the left side and bottom side sums are the same.)

NO, NO. I CAN'T GO THROUGH WITH IT!!! Just look the other way while I have my nervous breakdown. I can see now why algebra was invented. If you try to carry out computations with half words and things it ends up far more difficult to follow than algebra! Yes, it's harder to follow even than algebra!

So let's do it properly. Suppose that we can have entries x (top), y (left bottom) and z (right bottom). But suppose that we can also have circle entries of a, b and c in the same order. Then because the side sums are the same we get

$$a + b = x + y \qquad \dots (1)$$
$$b + c = y + z \qquad \dots (2)$$
$$c + a = z + x \qquad \dots (3)$$

Now subtract the second equation from the first and we get

$$a - c = x - z \qquad \dots (4)$$

Adding (4) and (3) we get

$$2a = 2x \quad \text{so} \quad a \text{ and } x \text{ are the same.}$$

The same fiddling around with the other terms gives $b = y$ and $c = z$. So this problem only has one answer! Wow, that's a relief.

And, seeing how I did that one, you can have a go now at the Four Circles problem to see why sometimes it doesn't have solutions and sometimes they aren't unique. What's more you might be able to extend the 3-gon algorithm to the 5-gon algorithm and even beyond.

It really does look as if there is a parity difference here. That is that even and odd sided polygons behave differently. It's all reminiscent of the 4×10^r Problem really.

▷ But it suddenly occurred to me that you might not have realised by now that all nice sets are of the form $\{a, b, c, a + d, b + d, c + d\}$. You should be able to see this from the last set of equations in the last chapter (see page 49). And now there is another question I can ask (you are not surprised?). We have found one nice set, {1, 2, 3, 4, 5, 6} that produces four blahs and another nice set {1, 2, 3, 4, 5, 7} that can only produce two blahs. What happens in general? Are there nice sets that only produce one, two, three, four or more blahs? What is especially nice about each of these possibilities?

6 *Scaffolding: a Means to an End*

I had a few window panes that were cracked and needed replacing. I'm living in an old two-storey house and it takes a long ladder to get to these windows. When I called in a glazier I was dismayed to hear that, under health and safety rules, it was necessary for him to have a scaffold to get up to the windows without risking life and limb. We discussed why he couldn't change the glass from the inside; maybe he could unscrew a few things, put the glass in and then screw the windows back again. Apparently the screws were rusted in and wouldn't turn. No, scaffolding was the only answer. Well at least it would get him where he wanted to go, but it was an extremely expensive way to change a few panes of glass.

Scaffolding in education comes free though, although it requires some effort. However, its purpose is the same as the material kind. The aim is to get someone where they couldn't get on his or her own, but I need to go back a step or two. It was Vygotsky who came up with the idea of the **zone of proximal development**. I've represented this diagrammatically below.

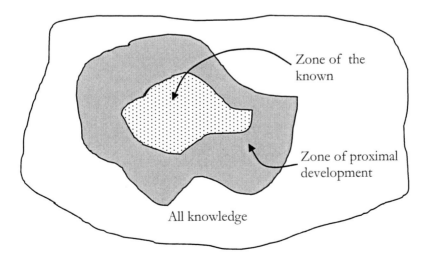

Figure 6.1 Knowledge zones.

In the space of all knowledge, an individual's knowledge takes up a small subset. What a person actually knows I'm going to call the **zone of the known**. Now around the edges of this is the **zone of proximal development** (zpd). That's the part of knowledge that the learner can reach with some assistance.

OK, now to get someone from their zone of the known to their zpd, we use **scaffolding**. This scaffolding can be facilitated in many different ways by many different people. So it can be achieved by questions, by conversation, by song, by pictures, and so on. And it can be produced both by knowledgeable people and not so knowledgeable people. While I was working on my PhD my wife frequently provided me with scaffolding. She knows very little about mathematics, but just by listening to what I had to say she helped me to understand the problem I was working on at that moment and somehow that created ideas that got me further up the mathematical building that I was trying to construct.

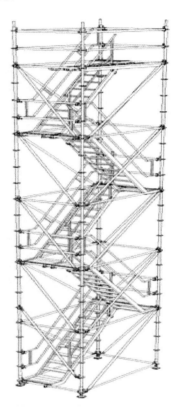

I've also seen students in a classroom scaffold each other too. Even though one had no idea how to do the problem they were working on, that student was still able to create scaffolding for their peer. This happens a lot and is a good reason for getting students to work together. This peer scaffolding I've also seen work time and time again in research groups. Clearly, no one in a research group knows how to solve the problem that the group is working on, but every now and again one person will say something that will light the bulb for a fellow researcher.

So we've covered the range of knowledgeable hierarchy from expert to peer to non-expert peer; there are people in each of these categories who can provide scaffolding wittingly or not, but you should also know that you can provide yourself with self-scaffolding.

Which is just as well or you'll never be able to solve a problem on your own.

As I've said before, there are many times when you are on your own and stuck with a problem that it would be nice to have someone at your shoulder to give you a bit of scaffolding at a vital moment. However, if there's never a good scaffolder around when you want one, then it's up to you to scaffold yourself.

But how is that possible?

> The important thing to notice about those pipes that form scaffolding is that they are separate from the building. They are not the building. The aim of scaffolding is to construct the building and then take the scaffolding away. The scaffolding is there to help **someone else** build the building.

This is important and fundamental. Actually, if you believe constructivists, you can't build someone else's knowledge for them anyway. So scaffolding for mathematics is **not** telling someone what the answer, the building, is. Scaffolding is facilitating knowledge construction. That someone else has to use the scaffolding. That means there is a two-way contract. I agree to help you by providing scaffolding. You agree to work on my scaffolding to increase your knowledge.

That was just a sneaky way of reminding you that to get much at all from this book, or from pretty well anything else for that matter, you have to do a lot of work. Incidentally, by breaking up this book into pieces by chevrons, I've tried to give you every opportunity to go off and work for yourself and not just rely on what I hope is my scaffolding. You might think about what scaffolding I've been giving, and how successful it has been.

- Oh, and are 'conjectures' scaffolding?

> It's actually very difficult to give examples of good scaffolding. Scaffolding almost always occurs in the heat of the battle between persons and problems. The strange thing too that I've found after looking at a lot of transcripts is that the participants in scaffolding often make sounds, gestures or drawings that seem unintelligible to anyone just looking on. However, somehow a few grunts or incomplete sentences might make all the difference for the scaffolding partner.

A great deal of scaffolding is particular to the precise situation of the moment. It's very hard to generalise. There is no universal scaffolding tool to be brought to bear on every situation. There are, however, a few questions that could be used at specific points of the problem-solving process. I'll run through some of these now and then go on to give a transcript of students scaffolding each other and their teacher. That last reference, to a student scaffolding a teacher, shouldn't worry you.

Can you think of an incident like that in your own experience? Hmm! That's not far from my wife scaffolding me.

What I want to do here is to divide the problem-solving process up into three parts and discuss the relevant scaffolding that might occur at each stage. Roughly I'll think of the stages, not very originally, as beginning, middle and end. Rather more originally and usually, a beginning, a muddle, and an end.

So what questions might be useful in the early stages of a problem? How about these?

- How would you get started on a problem like this?

- Can you rephrase this problem in your own words?

- What are the important ideas here?

- Have you seen a similar problem to this before?

- What information is given?

- What strategy might you use to get started?

- What experiments could you do?

If someone is in the middle of a problem then something like the following questions could be useful:

- Can you tell me what you are doing?

- Why are you doing it?

- Where might it get you when you've done it?

- Are you convinced that bit is correct?

- Have you tried looking at a simpler case?

In the latter stages of solving a problem the following could be valuable:

- Have you answered the problem?

- Have you considered all of the cases?

- Have you checked your solution? Does it look reasonable?

- Is there another answer?

- Is there another approach to the problem? Is it any simpler?

- Can you explain your method to me?

- Can you generalise the problem?

- Can you extend the problem?

- Can you make up a similar problem?

It might not be profitable for you to go back to see where I've asked these questions explicitly or implicitly in the previous chapters, but it might be worth being on the lookout for them in future. It might also be worth thinking about the questions you would have liked to have been asked when you were stuck.

What leading questions might have got you 'unstuck'?

 Now let's have a look at a student–student interaction. This is an actual transcript from a lesson.

Here L, K and S are students and T is the teacher. The problem that the students were working on was,

"What is the height of a stack of 1 million sheets of paper?".

To help the students they were given 500 sheets of paper. They measured the 500 sheets as being 5.8 cm thick. You will now appreciate what I said before about how disjointed real conversations can be.

1.	L:	(writing) 500 sheets. Height equals.
2.	K:	OK. Question 2.
3.	L:	Does everyone understand what we did with number one?
4.	K:	No, but, anyway, 500 sheets.
5.	L:	And how many sheets do we need?
6.	K:	500 sheets of what? 500 sheets.
7.	L:	Their height equals 5.8.
8.	S:	We've done that.
9.	K:	I know, but we've got to do it all together so.
10.	L:	One point oh times ten to the power of 6 divided by 500.
11.	K:	Oh yeah sure everyday, what are you talking about? What are you talking about?
12.	L:	I'm finding out how many 500s there are in a million.

13.	K:	How many 500s there are in a million? That would make it one thousand. How many 1000s are there in a million?
14.	K	That would make a 1000, 2000. What? (to S). I have a lot to say.
15.	L:	[checks result on calculator] 2000, well done!
16.	K:	This is called skill. This is what you do. 500 into 100 which is 2, then you do a 100 which is a 1000.
17.	L:	Times 5.8. Shush.
18.	K:	Which is 2? Then you do a thousand into a million, which is 1000, so a 1000 times two is 2000.
19.	L:	Eleven thousand six hundred.
20.	T:	With your working out folks I want you to tell me what you are mult – M – what you are multiplying by, and you simply put a little arrow telling me what and why.
21.	K:	What are we doing? Is it a million sheets of paper though?

I want to point out just a couple of lines here. In line 5 we see L asking a clarification question. Essentially she is asking what information is given in the problem. She would like to know the height of what particular number of sheets of paper they are looking for. In Line 11, K is seeking an explanation. This is a

" Can you tell me what you are doing ? "

question.

One thing to note here is that all of this is pretty natural. Nothing here is strange or mysterious. However, it's not clear that we always remember to ask these appropriate questions when we're by ourselves and in need of self-scaffolding.

Now for the students–teacher interaction. This problem concerns area and this is part of the transcript of an actual lesson.

1.	T:	Where'd you get 180 from?
2.	K:	Width. Equals 40.
3.	T:	Why did you multiply them together? Why not add?
4.	K:	To get the area. I know that much.
5.	T:	[to L] You've been tutoring her?
6.	K:	Equals forty-five thousand, therefore you'd need. Oh, how'd I get that?
7.	T:	Forty five thousand?
8.	K:	Forty-five thousand. That's what we got.
9.	T:	Forty-five thousand? Can you press that – can you press that – can you do that again? Two hundred and fifty times a hundred and eighty? Oh, hang on, hang on, I think you're right. Hang on. I think they're wrong.

Maybe Line 8 isn't classical scaffolding in that the student isn't leading the teacher on. However, by providing that answer, the teacher suddenly becomes aware that her own previous work was incorrect. Consequently she has been scaffolded to another answer (that may not necessarily have been the correct one).

I want to underline here that I don't see any problem with a teacher not knowing something (see the Introduction to this book). We can't all know everything. There is only a problem when a teacher doesn't know things on a regular basis.

And now I want to talk about staging points. It seems to me that all the problems I talk about in this book have natural places where you might want to stop. I call these **staging points**. These are places where a student has met their limit and is unable to go any further. The limit may be caused by them not knowing a particular piece of mathematics. For instance, a teacher may feel that a student's algebra is not sufficient for them to be able to produce, or even follow, the details of a proof. As a result, the teacher may be satisfied that it is good enough for that student to produce a reasonable conjecture.

I have made suggestions in Appendix II as to what the staging points for each problem in this book might be, but I'm sure that it is possible to interpret the steps of a problem in more than one way.

The staging point that a student can reach is a decision that has to be made by a teacher and is part of the scaffolding strategy that will be adopted.

Finally, here are some overall comments on scaffolding. To begin with, any act of scaffolding can possibly have two purposes. First, it is important for the situation in which it is being offered. So it has value 'for now'. But second, it is important for the future. There may well be a future occasion when that same scaffolding idea can be employed in another situation. This means that not only do you learn mathematical content as you go along, but you learn process ability, that is, a knowledge of how to work with content.

Then I want to underline that self-scaffolding is important and it is a fundamental part of all learning. After students have left school they will all meet problems. What's more many of these problems will be ones that they haven't met in school. This means that they have to have strategies to cope with these problems. Self-scaffolding is extremely valuable as an important strategy for later life. And this self-scaffolding can be used in areas other than mathematics.

Incidentally, I decided that scaffolding for my window panes was too expensive and so I found a glazier who would change glass panes without its use. He simply climbed a ladder – but I did have to pay for his mate to hold the ladder. I didn't mind because an hour or so of his mate's time was considerably less than the day of scaffolding that I would have had to pay for otherwise.

Much of this chapter can be found in Derek Holton and Gill Thomas *"Mathematical Interactions and Their Influence on Learning"* in David Clarke (ed.) *Perspectives on Practice and Meaning in Mathematics and Science Classrooms*, pp. 75–104, Dordrecht: Kluwer Academic, 2001

There are 21 cubes on the table. Alice and Blair take alternate turns at removing one or two cubes at a time. The winner is the one who takes the last cube.

On the principle of 'ladies first', Alice always takes the first turn. Does Alice have a winning strategy? Does Blair have a winning strategy? Or is who will win all a matter of luck?

▷ Proof is an essential part of mathematics, but it's often hard to convince students of its importance and to see its necessity. However, **combinatorial games** afford an area in which a proot can justify a strategy and so produce a winning way. Unfortunately in this chapter I will do more talking about proof than actually proving anything. You on the other hand …

But what are combinatorial games? Roughly speaking they are games between two players who take turns to play. Furthermore, they are games where there is always complete information to both players. Noughts and Crosses is a combinatorial game, but anything involving dice or cards usually isn't because there is never complete information to both players. The combinatorial game I want to explore here is the 21 Game, a form of 'Nim'. I'll get to Nim later. As we shall see, though, someone has a winning strategy, but it depends more on the 21 than it does on Alice or Blair.

With this kind of problem it's always a good idea to play the game to get a feel for what's going on. It's better to do this with someone else than to play against yourself because you can discuss strategies and try to see whether it's likely that Alice, the first player, always wins or always loses, or whatever. However, my experience in the classroom suggests that often just playing the game leads to no conclusions. Generally speaking, players win or lose seemingly randomly and so they can't see any winning strategy for anyone. The one thing though that playing the game does do is to ensure that students get a full understanding of the rules.

I'll have a coffee while you go off and play. Oh and don't forget about self-scaffolding.

▷ The thing that I find hard to get across to students is that there might possibly be a winning strategy for either Alice or Blair. The idea that one person may be able to force a win no matter what the other player does, appears to be totally contradictory to their previous experience, both in this game and elsewhere in life. Mostly they put the results down to chance. At this point I go back to Noughts and Crosses to show them that, if either player is playing as well as possible, the game must end up as a draw, but, especially with younger students, even this seems a surprise.

Having tried something that you know and is a bit like this problem, its time for a new problem solving strategy – try a **smaller case**. Somehow, 21 is too big and in the early stages it's too hard to see the game for the cubes.

So what if there was only **one cube**?
(You can't get a smaller case than this.)
Surely Alice must always win?

The same goes for **two cubes** because Alice can take two cubes when it's her turn.

But **three cubes** is a different kettle of fish:
- if Alice takes one cube,
  Blair takes two and wins;
- if Alice takes two cubes,
  Blair takes one and wins.

What's going to happen with four cubes?
- If Alice takes one cube, Blair is in the same position as Alice was in the previous case. So he now loses;
- on the other hand, if Alice takes two cubes, Blair can remove the two that are left and he wins.

At first sight this suggests that there is no good strategy for either player; and that either can win depending on how Alice starts. But that's the whole point. Alice surely *wants* to win. So why should she start in a way that allows Blair to win? Surely Alice will take one cube and watch Blair suffer rather than take two and face the possibility of losing?

Have a look at the five-cube case. Can you see that Alice has a winning strategy?

At this point it looks as if Alice will always win. Apart from the three-cube situation, being first player puts her in a strong position and she should never lose. Perhaps we could dismiss three as a case of the law of small numbers – with small numbers anything can happen because there's just not enough room to manoeuvre.

But six is a Blair win! Whether Alice takes one or two cubes, Blair can make sure that after his move there are only three cubes left, and, if Alice is faced with three cubes, Blair can force a win.

So that begins to suggest we have a pattern on our hands. (It might be an idea to draw up a table about now.) As far as Alice is concerned three and six are bad numbers. Isn't it likely that nine and 12 and, well, any multiple of three are bad numbers for her? That means that provided Blair plays "properly", he will always win the 21 Game. And "properly" means that all he has to do is to take Alice down to the next multiple of three at each stage!

Of course we can't leave it there. Who decided that Alice and Blair could only take one or two cubes? What happens if they are allowed to take one, two or even three cubes a time from the group of 21? What numbers are good for Alice and what for Blair?

▷ Let's analyse this game (I assume that you've done some work on the extended problem before you started reading this section), make a conjecture and then try to prove the conjecture. It's pretty obvious that with only one, two or three cubes, that under the new rules Alice must win. Does she still win with four cubes? Well, no. No matter which of her three options she takes, Blair can take the rest of the cubes when it's his turn.

Hmm. Is it likely then that multiples of 4 are bad for Alice? Check out a few more possibilities and see how it looks. So where do we go next? Suppose that Alice and Blair have *n* cubes on the table and the possibility of removing up to four cubes at a turn. That should provide you with an obvious conjecture.

At this stage we have to go the whole hog. Start with *n* cubes. Let Alice and Blair take their choice of up to *r* cubes when it's their turn. This leads us to the following conjecture.

Conjecture: Let n be the number of cubes at the start of play. Suppose Alice and Blair can take up to r cubes on their turn. If they both play optimally, then:

- $n = a(r + 1)$ is bad for Alice (where a is any whole number)
- all other numbers are bad for Blair.

▷ Now have you noticed what's going on here? Once we have solved the original 21 Game, with $r = 2$, we can move towards a generalisation of the game where Alice and Blair are allowed to take up to r cubes away at a time from the original n cubes.

Unfortunately we can't do that kind of development with all problems. If you remember the first situation where this was not possible was in Chapter 1 with the 400 Problem. This isn't too bad as you can make considerable progress, but what becomes the 4×10^r Problem does lurch from r being even to r being odd. Then it happens again in the Difference Problem of Chapter 2 where strange things start to happen as the number of digits increases. Anyway we'll enjoy it while we can. But maybe you should spend a while trying to prove the last Conjecture.

▷ I want to change tacks a little here. With just a minor change to the original 21 Game we can get something else that's worth thinking about. Alice and Blair were playing to see who could take the last cube. Change things around by making the person who takes the last cube the loser! This is known as the **misère** version of the game. You might like to see what numbers are bad for Alice in this version of the game. Start with $r = 2$ and hope that, whatever you get there, both the bad numbers and the proofs will generalise upward. Well don't just hope, check it out!

▷ But we can keep going in several directions with this problem. Let's now talk about the game of Nim. Here the cubes are placed arbitrarily in two or more groups - it will become obvious why the 1-group game isn't very interesting.

When it's their turn Alice and Blair can take any number (at least one) of cubes they like provided they all come from one group. The winner again, is the one who takes (is forced to take) the last cube. Let's play a game. Below we have ten cubes in two groups.

Figure 7.1   Nim with ten cubes in 2 groups.

What should Alice do? If she takes all of the cubes from one of the groups, Blair will take all of the cubes from the remaining group. So taking all of the cubes from one group is not a good idea for her.

What if Alice takes all but one cube from a group? Blair doesn't dare to take that lone cube because Alice will then take all of the cubes from the other group. So what should Blair do?

Play Nim, analyse it, and see what you come up with. The questions that then arise are, does Alice have a winning strategy? Does Blair have a winning strategy? And does this depend on the number of cubes in one group or both groups?

 How did you go with the misère version of the original 21 Game? Alice is playing first and can take one or two cubes at a time, but, to win, she must force Blair to take the last cube. My guess is that she'd be pretty unhappy if there was only one cube, but more than satisfied if there were two or three cubes. Suppose we call numbers in the misère version **m-bad** for Alice if she loses when that number of cubes is on the table. Then it looks as if 4 is the next *m*-bad number after 1. If Alice removes *i*, for *i* = 1, 2, then Blair removes 3 − *i* to leave Alice with a cube she can't refuse. Doesn't that look as if $n = 3k + 1$ is *m*-bad for Alice? And now we have come up with a conjecture you should try to prove it.

Almost certainly, if our two players can remove up to *r* cubes at a time, then we'll find that

$$n = a(r + 1) + 1 \text{ is } m\text{-bad}$$

for Alice and maybe you can prove it. Well you can if it's

correct, if you can't, then what is correct? I'd be inclined to try a few more values of *r* before you got too excited with my conjecture though.

▷ And that takes us back to regular old Nim again. How did you go with ten cubes in 2 groups? What if Alice took two cubes from the bigger group to make them both equal at four a piece? What would/could Blair do?

Well Blair won't reduce any group to one (Alice will reduce the other group to one). And he's not likely to take all of one group (Alice will take all of the other group). So Blair leaves two or three cubes on one of the groups. I'll analyse the first of these situations and I'll leave you to work on the other one.

So let's suppose that Blair has taken two cubes from one group. What should Alice do? With a bit of work you should see that the best option Alice has is to remove two from the other group. That leaves Blair fixed to either leave one cube in a group or no cubes in a group. Alice can surely win this way.

Does that mean that, if the game starts off with two unequal groups, Alice can win by making them equal? But what should she do if the two groups had an equal number of cubes to start off with? Is she doomed from the very start?

And when you've absorbed that, what happens if there are three or more groups? Suppose Alice and Blair had groups of six, seven and eight cubes. Would Alice win or not? Is there a general strategy for tackling Nim with an arbitrary number of cubes in an arbitrary number of groups?

You can now see that there is no end to the problems that mathematicians have to worry about! And in that vein of thinking, think about this one. How does Alice go about tackling the original 21 Game if there were two groups instead of one? What about three groups instead of two? What about *s* groups with *n* cubes in total and Alice and Blair can take up to *r* cubes from any given group when it's their turn? And the one who takes the last cube wins.

Let's start this off with *r* = *s* = 2. Suppose again we had six cubes in one group and four in another. What should Alice do? What should Blair do?

Hmmmm! In retrospect, it might be easier to take $r = s = 2$ where the two groups are of equal size. For small group sizes we might be able to analyse what could happen. In the diagrams below I've done that for group sizes of one, two, three and four. Is there a pattern here? I hope the notation isn't too cryptic. The idea is that the first number in the brackets is the number of cubes in the first group and similarly for the second number and the second group. Who takes what is shown by the arrows.

It's pretty simple starting with one cube in each group

$$(1, 1) \xrightarrow{A} (0, 1) \xrightarrow{B} (0, 0)$$

Blair wins

Starting with two cubes in each group leads to the same conclusion, when we make use of the last result:

$$(2, 2) \begin{cases} \xrightarrow{A} (2, 1) \xrightarrow{B} (1, 1) \\ \\ \xrightarrow{A} (2, 0) \xrightarrow{B} (0, 0) \end{cases}$$

Blair wins

Starting with three cubes, and making use of each of the two previous result, leads to the same conclusion:

$$(3, 3) \begin{cases} \xrightarrow{A} (3, 2) \xrightarrow{B} (2, 2) \\ \\ \xrightarrow{A} (3, 1) \xrightarrow{B} (1, 1) \end{cases}$$

Blair wins

and again with four cubes:

$$(4, 4) \begin{cases} \xrightarrow{A} (4, 3) \xrightarrow{B} (3, 3) \\ \\ \xrightarrow{A} (4, 2) \xrightarrow{B} (2, 2) \end{cases}$$

Blair wins

In every case Blair wins. So it looks as if it's not worth Alice's while to play this game. Does she do better with the misère version?

About now you may want to look up Nim and its various ramifications on the web. On the other hand, there are some good books on combinatorial games that you might want to read too.

Just in case you think I've talked about all possible games of this type you might want to think about (i) Nim, but the player who takes the last cube loses, the misère version; or (ii) the original 21 Game, in either normal or misère form, where there are more than two groups and not all groups have the same number of cubes.

That ought to keep you out of mischief for a while!

8   *Induction: a Method of Proof*

Informally in the last chapter I introduced the method of proof called **Mathematical Induction**. I want to cover it more formally in this chapter.

Dominoes have been all the rage, not so much as a game, but as objects to push over! If you line up domino pieces in a row, standing up as they are in the drawing below, a simple push at the point *A* on the left-most domino will cause each domino in turn to fall.

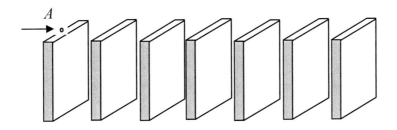

Many people put a great deal of effort into lining up domino pieces so that they fall in all sorts of interesting ways. When I had a quick look at the internet while I was writing this, I noticed a world record claim for the linked collapse of over 4 million dominoes.

Some of these tumblings involved objects other than domino pieces. It may be worth a look on the web to see how involved these 'fallings' are. This notion of falling dominoes was so common that it led to the **Domino Theory** in international politics that was used particularly by countries opposed to communism. The idea was to stop country *A* from being subject to communist rule, as this would make it less likely for country *B* to become communist and so on for countries *C, D*, etc.

Falling dominoes are a graphic example of the proof technique called **Mathematical Induction**. Before I say any more about this technique let me talk about how to program a robot to climb a ladder.

Obviously the robot won't be in a climbing position until it is on the ladder so the first thing that needs to be done is to actually get the robot onto the ladder. If you can then show it how to go from any given rung to the next rung you'll have yourself a ladder-climbing robot. To convince you of this, imagine putting the robot on the first rung. Because the robot can go from any rung to the next it can get to the second rung. Because it can go from any rung to the next it can get to the third rung. Because …

If we can start the robot; if it can get as far as some rung, say the *k*-th one; and if we can get it from the *k*-th rung to the next rung; then it will climb the ladder.

In the same way, if the dominoes are lined up so that the *k*-th one will knock over the (*k* + 1)-th one for all *k*, then they will all fall over once we have knocked the first one onto the second one. We have to be sure that the first one will knock over the second one and then the rest will all fall down by the *k* to *k* + 1 argument.

This is essentially what Mathematical Induction does for some mathematical situations where we need a proof for all integers from a certain point on. You just need to follow the steps below.

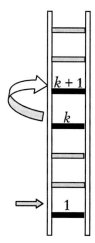

Step 1. *Show that the situation has the property we want for the number 1.*

Step 2. *Assume that the situation has the property we want for some fixed number k.*

Step 3. *Prove that the situation has the property we want for the next number k + 1.*

And the proof works just like a robot ascending a ladder. If the property holds for the number one; if the property holds up to the number *k*; and if we can get up to the number *k* + 1; then we can show the property holds for all numbers. It works because we can start at one. Then with $k = 1$ we can prove we can get to $k + 1 = 2$. But with $k = 2$ we can prove we can get to $k + 1 = 3$. But with $k = 3$ we can prove $\cdots$. On and on and on forever and for all positive integers.

There are, of course, a number of forms of Mathematical Induction. For example, we may have to start at some whole number higher than 1 in Step 1 and we may want to assume that all numbers up to and including k have the required property.

I'm now going to take Mathematical Induction and show that every multiple of 3 is bad for Alice in the original 21 Game. Remember that Alice goes first and then she and Blair take turns to remove one or two blocks from the pile. A number is bad for Alice if she can be made to lose when she and Blair are playing with that number of blocks.

Theorem 1 $3t$ is bad for Alice, where t is any positive integer.

Proof   I'll do the Mathematical Induction on t and this will produce the result that every multiple of 3 is bad for Alice.

Step 1.   First I have to show the situation holds for $t = 1$. We've actually seen this in the last chapter but I'll do it again.

With three blocks if Alice takes one, then Blair will take two and win. On the other hand, if Alice takes two, Blair will take one and win. So three ($t = 1$) is bad for Alice.

Step 2.   All I have to do here is to assume that $3t$ is bad for some arbitrary value of t, k say.

Step 3.   Now I have to show that if $3k$ is bad for Alice then so is $3(k + 1)$. Suppose then I have $3(k + 1)$ blocks. What I'm going to show is that Blair can force the pile to just $3k$ blocks. From there we know Blair can win by Step 2. That will then mean that $3(k + 1)$ is bad for Alice. So $t = k + 1$ works and we have completed our proof by Mathematical Induction.

OK then, I have $t = k + 1$ and $3(k + 1) = 3k + 3$ blocks. If Alice removes one block, Blair removes two and they are down to $3k$ blocks. Alice loses from here by Step 2.

If Alice removes two blocks, Blair removes one and they are down to $3k$ blocks. Again Alice loses from here by Step 2.

I've shown then that for $t = k + 1$, Alice loses. $3(k + 1)$ is bad for her. Now by the Principle of Mathematical Induction $3t$ is bad for Alice for all positive integer values of t.

You might like to go through the extended game where the players can take one, two or three blocks away. Prove, by Mathematical Induction, that $4t$ is bad for Alice there.

But then what is stopping you proving that $(r + 1)t$ is bad for Alice in the game where $1, 2, \ldots, r-1$ or r blocks can be removed at any time.

Now theorems only do what they say they do - just like labels on a tin. The theorem I have just proved says that $3t$ is bad for Alice. It doesn't tell us what is bad for Blair! Maybe, despite our previous experience, nothing is bad for him. Whatever the situation is, Theorem 1 doesn't tell us that at all. How can we prove then that every number that is *not* a multiple of 3 is bad for poor old Blair?

Theorem 2 Let n be a number that is not a multiple of 3. Then n is bad for Blair.

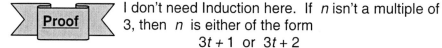

Proof I don't need Induction here. If n isn't a multiple of 3, then n is either of the form
$$3t + 1 \text{ or } 3t + 2$$
because when you divide n by 3 you either get a remainder of 1 or 2. We consider each of these possibilities separately.

Suppose $n = 3t + 1$. Alice confidently removes one block from the pile of $3t + 1$ blocks. It now has $3t$ blocks. If $t = 0$, then Alice has already won. If not, from **Theorem I**, I know that $3t$ is bad for the first player who tackles a pile of $3t$ blocks. Blair has that privilege. He is doomed to lose. So $3t + 1$ is bad for Blair.

Now suppose $n = 3t + 2$ and it is Alice's turn again. She takes two blocks and Blair is in trouble.

So $3t + 2$ as well as $3t + 1$ is bad for Blair. End of story!

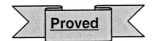

Proved

Well - not quite. You might like to note that we can combine Theorems 1 & 2 to show that Blair wins if and only if $n = 3t$.

From here you can clean up the other one-pile extensions of the 21 Game as well as its generalisation to removing up to r blocks at a time. The misère version should now also hold no problems for you.

I'm going to do two more examples of Mathematical Induction. The first one will be a textbook exercise and the second a proof of the existence part of the 4×10^r Problem.

OK. Now we're armed for the second problem. What factors does

$$n^3 - n$$

have no matter what whole number n we use? Clearly we need to experiment. I'll put the results of my experimenting in a table.

n	1	2	3	4	5	6	7	8	9
$n^3 - n$	0	6	24	60	120	210	336	504	720

A quick check shows that 6 seems to go into all of them. 12 is a factor of a lot – but it doesn't divide the $n = 2$, 6 or 10 cases. So let's guess that 6 is a factor of $n^3 - n$ no matter what value n has.

Proof

Let's see if we can prove that using Mathematical Induction.

Step 1. Is 6 a factor of $1^3 - 1 = 0$? Well, $0 = 6 \times 0$ so since 6 divides the right side of that equation it must divide the left. Yes, 6 is a factor of $1^3 - 1$.

Step 2. Assume that $k^3 - k$ is divisible by 6 for some fixed value of k. This means that $k^3 - k$ is a multiple of 6 and hence that $k^3 - k = 6s$ for some whole number s.

Step 3.   Now we have to show that 6 divides $(k+1)^3 - (k+1)$.

$$(k+1)^3 - (k+1) = k^3 + 3k^2 + 3k + 1 - k - 1$$
$$= k^3 - k + 3k^2 + 3k$$
$$= (k^3 - k) + 3k(k+1).$$

Now I've deliberately split the right side of the equation into two separate bits because I want to tackle each one separately. Fine.

First, let's look at $k^3 - k$. By Step 2 I know that this is $6s$ for some s.

Second, let's look at $3k(k+1)$. Now this is obviously divisible by 3 because there is a factor of 3 sitting out in front. What I need to be able to do now is to show that $k(k+1)$ is divisible by 2. But that's not hard. The numbers k and $k+1$ are consecutive. That means that one of them is always even (and one is always odd). The even one will give us the factor of 2 we need. Hence $3k(k+1) = 6t$ for some number t.

Putting these two bits together gives

$$(k+1)^3 - k = 6s + 6t = 6(s+t).$$

Just what I wanted: $(k+1)^3 - k$ is divisible by 6. I have proved the following theorem by Mathematical Induction.

Proved

> **Theorem 3** Let n be any whole number then $n^3 - n$ is always divisible by 6.

Now you've seen how to do that you might like to explore the factors of $n^3 - n + 24$, $n^3 - n^2$ and $n^4 - n$ and any others that you care to experiment with.

There are a couple of things I want to say now. The first is about the last problem and the second about Induction in general.

Actually there is another, more revealing, way to prove that $n^3 - n$ is divisible by 6. Factorise!

$$n^3 - n = n(n^2 - 1) = n(n-1)(n+1) = (n-1)n(n+1).$$

Putting it in that last form shows that $n^3 - n$ is always made up of **three** consecutive numbers: $n - 1$, n and $n + 1$.

Clearly, from what I said above one of these numbers must be even and that gives me my factor of 2. But in any **three** consecutive numbers there must be one that has a factor of 3. So

$$(n - 1)n(n + 1)$$

has both a factor of 2 and a factor of 3. Hence it must have a factor of 6.

You might like to think about which values of n force

$$n^3 - n$$

to have a factor of 12.

And now my comment about Mathematical Induction. Some people worry about the second step.   It's the 'assume' that worries them. Aren't we assuming what we are trying to prove? The answer there is "yes" and "no", so that obviously makes it OK! Let me try that again. We are sort of assuming what we're trying to prove but it's OK. Why? Well, for the robot-ladder-climbing and domino-falling reasons. By the time we get to use Step 2 it *is* true.

Let's look at it more formally this way. You have a proposition that concerns a number n and you want to show that that proposition is true for 'all values of n'. Usually this means 'for all $n \geq 1$' but occasionally it's 'for all $n \geq 0$' and, rarer still, 'for all n greater than or equal to some specified starting value other than 0 or 1'. Let's denote the proposition by the symbol P(n).

Step 1 shows that P(1) is true. We now *know* that there are values of n for which P(n) is true since we've found one, namely $n = 1$. This is *not* an *assumption*.

Step 2 then continues the argument as follows. Suppose k is a value of n for which the proposition P(n) is true. (Again we *know* we can find one.).

Step 3 then proves that, from our known starting points, $k + 1$ is also a value of n for which P(n) is true. And that completes the inductive argument since all the numbers greater than or equal to 1 become possible choices for n.

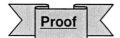

The final step here is to prove the 4×10^r Problem has a solution 3, 6, 3, 6, ..., 3, 6, for r even. This proof is a but I've completed it to show that it can be done. Have a quick flip through the first time. Come back to it again some time later.

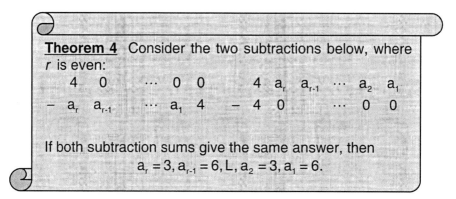

Theorem 4 Consider the two subtractions below, where r is even:

$$
\begin{array}{cccccc}
4 & 0 & \cdots & 0 & 0 \\
- & a_r & a_{r-1} & \cdots & a_1 & 4
\end{array}
\qquad
\begin{array}{cccccc}
4 & a_r & a_{r-1} & \cdots & a_2 & a_1 \\
- & 4 & 0 & \cdots & 0 & 0
\end{array}
$$

If both subtraction sums give the same answer, then
$$a_r = 3, a_{r-1} = 6, L, a_2 = 3, a_1 = 6.$$

Proof   I'll let $r = 2v$ and do my Induction on v.

Step 1.   The theorem is true for $v = 1$. Now I'm not actually going to do this because it's the 400 Problem and that's been done already in Chapter 1. So I'm going to assume this is OK.

Step 2.   Assume the theorem is true for $v = k$.

Step 3.   I now have to show/prove that the following two subtractions are equal when $a_{2k+2} = 3$, $a_{2k+1} = 6$, ..., $a_2 = 3$, $a_1 = 6$.

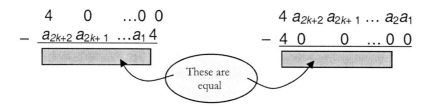

I have to do this by somehow appealing to Step 2. What I'm going to do then, is to break up the two subtractions. Start with the first subtraction:

$$
\begin{array}{r}
4 \quad 0 \quad \ldots \quad 0\ 0 \\
-\ a_{2k+2}\ a_{2k+1}\ \ldots\ a_1\ 4 \\
\hline
\end{array}
\Longrightarrow
\begin{array}{r}
4 \quad 0 \quad \ldots \quad 0\ 0\ 0\ 0 \\
-\ a_{2k+2}\ a_{2k+1}\ \ldots\ a_3\ a_2 a_1 4 \\
\hline
\end{array}
$$

$$
\Longrightarrow
\begin{array}{r}
4 \quad 0 \quad \ldots \quad 0\ 0\ 0\ 0 \\
-\ a_{2k+2}\ a_{2k+1}\ \ldots\ a_3\ a_2\ 0\ 0 \\
\hline
\end{array}
\quad \text{and} \quad
\begin{array}{r}
0\ 0 \\
-\ a_1\ 4 \\
\hline
\end{array}
$$

$$
\Longrightarrow
\begin{array}{r}
4 \quad 0 \quad \ldots \quad 0\ 0\ 0\ 0 \\
-\ a_{2k+2} a_{2k+1}\ \ldots\ a_3\ 4\ 0\ 0 \\
\hline
\end{array}
\quad \text{and} \quad
\begin{array}{r}
1\ 0\ 0 \\
-\ a_1\ 4 \\
\hline
\end{array}
$$

with a **balance** of $(4 - a_2 - 1) \times 100$.

Note the balance. I've taken 100 off the left part; I've ignored a_2; and I've stuck -400 in. So I need to add $(4 - a_2 - 1) \times 100$ at the end.

And now for the second sum

$$
\begin{array}{r}
4 a_{2k+2}\ a_{2k+1}\ \ldots\ a_2\ a_1 \\
-4\ 0 \quad\ 0\ \ldots\ 0\ 0 \\
\hline
\end{array}
$$

$$
\Longrightarrow
\begin{array}{r}
4 a_{2k+2}\ a_{2k+1}\ \ldots\ a_3\ 0\ 0 \\
-4\ 0 \quad\ 0\ \ldots\ 0\ 0\ 0 \\
\hline
\end{array}
\quad \text{and} \quad
\begin{array}{r}
a_2\ a_1 \\
-0\ 0 \\
\hline
\end{array}
$$

Now you have to remember that the two broken pieces with the 'and' in between give the same subtraction.

To get any further I want to concentrate on the two end bits

$$
\begin{array}{r}
1\ 0\ 0 \\
-\quad a_1\ 4 \\
\hline
\end{array}
\quad \text{and} \quad
\begin{array}{r}
a_2\ a_1 \\
-0\ 0 \\
\hline
\end{array}
$$

Now I complete these as far as I can easily go:

$$
\begin{array}{r}
1 0\ 0 \\
-\ a_1\ 4 \\
\hline
6 \\
\end{array}
\quad \text{and} \quad
\begin{array}{r}
a_2\ a_1 \\
-\ 0\ 0 \\
\hline
a_2\ a_1 \\
\end{array}
$$

Since the two sums are equal, $a_1 = 6$. Then

$$\begin{array}{r} 100 \\ - \ \ 64 \\ \hline 36 \end{array}$$

gives $a_2 = 3$.

That a_2 is 3 is marvellous. That means that our balance

$$(4 - a_2 - 1) \times 100$$

is just nothing, zero, 0. So we can ignore the balance and look at the rest of the parts.

$$\begin{array}{r} 4 \quad 0 \quad \ldots \ 0 \ 000 \\ - \ a_{2k+2} \ a_{2k+1} \quad \ldots \ a_3 \ 400 \end{array} \qquad \begin{array}{r} 4 \ a_{2k+2} \ a_{2k+1} \ \ldots \ a_3 \ 00 \\ - \ 4 \quad 0 \quad \ 0 \ \ldots \quad 0 \ 00 \end{array}$$

From Step 2 we know that $a_{2k+2} = 3$, $a_{2k+1} = 6$, $a_{2k} = 3$, $a_{2k-1} = 6$, $\cdots$ $a_4 = 3$, $a_3 = 6$. We already know that $a_2 = 3$, and $a_1 = 6$ so we have proved the theorem.

Proved

(But it's not a *nice* proof! Don't you think it's *worse* than the algebraic proof?)

The theorem says that if r is even and the two subtractions are equal we get the solution with threes and sixes. But it is also true that if r is even and we put the threes and sixes in the appropriate places, then the two subtractions are equal. So we have a characterisation here and we can re-write the statement of the theorem with an **if and only if**.

If you have any strength left you might like to see how this works for the 5×10^2 Problem and then the $n \times 10^r$ Problem with r even. Can you do the r odd case by Induction?

9   *The Frogs Problem*

Suppose that we have three boy frogs ⬜ sitting on three lily pads

and three girl frogs ▦ sitting on another three lily pads.

In all, there are seven lily pads in a row with the boy frogs and girl frogs at either end and a spare lily pad in the middle. Frogs can move by sliding to an adjacent empty lily pad or by jumping over one other frog to an empty lily pad.

The boy frogs must always keep moving to the end where the girl frogs started and vice versa. Can the boys end up in the girls' original positions and the girls end up in the boys' original positions? If so, what is the smallest number of moves that it takes? If not, why not?

This problem is sometimes stated in terms of yaks or kangaroos. But the full extent of the problem is often not explored. As I hope you will shortly see, there is more to this problem than meets the eye.

I like to do the problem with 'live frogs'. I get three boys and three girls to sit in the appropriate positions in seven chairs at the front of the class. Then I appoint a 'frog master' or two to direct the frogs. However, I usually find that before long other students get involved, and even the frogs themselves want a say in the action.

Three frogs a side is just enough to make the problem non-trivial. To make it really interesting you might jump straight into eight frogs a side, but let's hold that for the moment. For now, let me take a break while you have a go at the Frog Problem. Try it out at:

http://www2.nzmaths.co.nz/frames/brightsparks/frogs.asp?applet

Generalise and extend, and justify everything.

One reason why I keep stopping to let you try the problems out is that you will never realise how hard these problems are, or what subtleties they hold, unless you have a go at them for yourself. If you see any problem in its solved state for the first time you'll generally believe that it's easy and won't appreciate the work involved in solving it.

What's more, by trying the problems you will understand the rules better and see why certain things are part of the question. Having a go will also help you tremendously to take a full part in the discussions that I try to hold here and hopefully help you to see why I have gone down certain paths but not others.

So it's important to have a go. I don't mind if you get the problems out or not, but I will mind if you don't try them.

It doesn't take long for the rules to be absorbed and for the students to see what it is that blocks progress. However, it sometimes takes several attempts before most of the class get on top of the process. I generally get various frog masters to run the frogs before I'm satisfied that everyone has a pretty good idea of what is going on.

The key to the process is that it's best not to get two frogs of the same gender next to each other unless you're at the final stages of the solution. If you can keep this in your head, then you're likely to put the right moves together and swap the frogs over.

It's important to realise that there is more than one way to do this problem. But don't despair: they are symmetric. Letting a boy frog go first gives essentially the same set of moves as letting a girl frog hop off at the start.

Don't expect this symmetry to hold in all of the problems involving frogs here though.

Anyway, here is *a* method of solving the original problem.

There were two parts to the question and the diagram answers only one of them. Yes we can see that the swap can be achieved. But I'll leave for the moment the question of whether the 15 moves here is the smallest number of moves that will produce the swap.

At this stage I usually ask the students if it's possible to do the same thing with four, five, six or *f* frogs of each gender?

- If it's possible, how many moves will it take?
- If it's not possible what can stop it happening?

Here's where I leave you for the old coffee while you do a bit of experimenting. But before you do, what do you think will happen? Can we get the swap for any number of frogs of each persuasion? If not, why not? If so, how, and how many moves will it take to effect the swap?

Again I don't mind if you are right or not. I just think the mental exercise sharpens your intuition and helps you to think in future. You may also be aware of some false moves when you are doing this problem with others

 You know by now that I hop off on a tangent any chance I get, so here is my first frog tangent. You're beginning to think that you can do this problem and that, given time, you could do it for all values of *f*, the number of frogs of each gender. But when you think about it there is no reason why we should have the same number of frogs on either side. What would happen if we had *b* boy frogs and *g* girls frogs? Ask the usual questions:

- Is it possible?
- If it isn't, why isn't it?
- If it is, how many moves will be needed?

It's time to experiment again. Oh and don't go looking a few sections ahead to see how it turns out. Do your own hard work.

That reminds me of a quote I once came across that went something like this:

The one who does the thinking does the learning.

But it's certainly true that you'll get more out of this book by working at the problems.

OK, so if we go back to the *f* a side game, here's what I think is going on so far, where *N* is the number of frog moves.

f	1	2	3	4	5	6	7
N	3	8	15	24	35	48	63

- **Is there a pattern?**
- **If so, what is it?**

It seems that students are geared up to looking at the difference between numbers. They soon see that these differences are

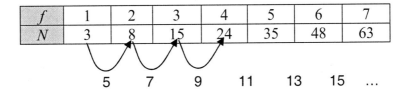

That pattern is clear. Using that they can keep the table going for ever and many of them are contented with that, especially the primary students who haven't really met formulae at that stage. But it's often hard for them to see how to convert the differences into an expression for *N*.

It usually doesn't take long for secondary classes to come up with

$$f(f+2)$$

although it seems to arrive directly from looking at the positions of the numbers in the table. If $f = 2$, then $f + 2$ is two across the row and is equal to 4. And the value of *N* at $f = 2$ is 4×2. The same thing seems to be happening for every value of *f* in the table.

For some reason the pattern

$$(f+1)^2 - 1$$

is not so obvious to them. This is probably because one less than a square is not something they commonly experience.

We can't just accept the formula on the basis of 'pattern spotting'. Why not ? In Chapter 17 we look at the **Regions' problem** and spot a pattern. The problem is, the pattern breaks down spectacularly the very next time. So we have to have a proof. But finding a proof is not easy; I'll come back to that in the next chapter.

At first sight there is no good reason why it should be possible to switch *b* boy frogs with *g* girl frogs for any reasonable values of *b* and *g*. But for *b* = 2 and *g* = 3 it surely does work and it also does for the other values in the table a little further on. Anyway, here's *b* = 2 and *g* = 3 working two non-symmetrical ways. (But are they really different?)

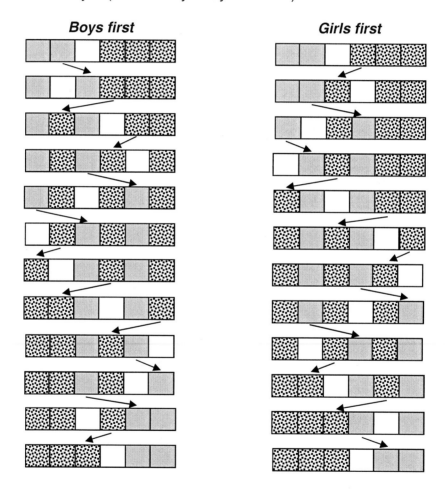

Boys first　　　　　　　**Girls first**

The thing to notice here is that there are actually two seemingly different ways to put together the 11 moves (but remember - there are 12 arrangements of frogs) that will change the frogs over. It depends on whether you have a "ladies first" philosophy or not. I can't see any obvious reason as to why they both do the job in the same number of moves. (And maybe that isn't true.)

Anyway, here's the table I promised.

b	2	2	2	3	3	3	4	4	4
g	3	4	5	4	5	6	5	6	7
N	11	14	17	19	23	27	29	34	39

- **Can you get any patterns from that ?**

Incidentally it has suddenly occurred to me that the number of moves of each type, **jumps** and **slides** might be worth knowing. Oh, a jump is when one frog moves over a given frog to the next empty lily pad

and a slide is just a move to the next empty lily pad

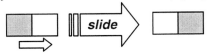

There just may be some value in these jump and slide numbers. My conjecture for the f frog-a-side case is that there are

$$f^2 \text{ jumps}$$

and

$$2f \text{ slides.}$$

Do you agree with that?

I'll let you produce your own conjectures for the b and g situations. However, whatever you get for b and g should be the same as you get for f when you let $b = f = g$.

▷ And here's my second tangent. In fact I can think of at least one more. But this one I'll call the **Frogs LS problem**. You'll see why in a moment. What if the boys have stronger back legs than the girls? So what if when the boys jump, they can only jump over two frogs onto an empty lily pad? They can slide OK, but they can't make the smaller jumps that we have been thinking about so far. So in Frogs LS, the L stands for long jumps and the S for short jumps.

This problem seems to be more problematic. I don't think that there is an obvious algorithm here as there is with the original Frogs Problem. Let's start with the *f* frogs-a-side situation, so there are equal numbers on either side. Let me do an example.

Suppose $f = 3$.

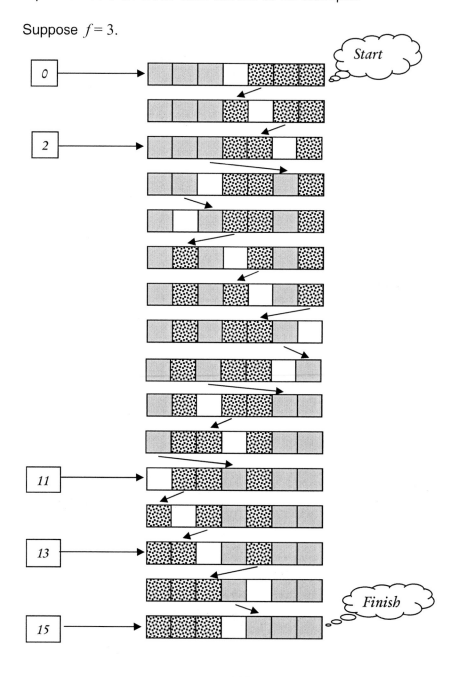

First of all, it's nice to know that it can be done. However, it's a little surprising that it takes as many moves with some long-legged jumps in there as it did with all the short-legged jumps. I would have expected long legs to have **saved** some moves. Where have I gone wrong?

Ah hang on! It took me two 'girl' slides to get from line 0 to line 2 above. But if I do a 'girl' jump I can skip line 1. In the same way, I can skip line 12. That brings the number here down to 13 moves. If I thought a bit more about it, it's possible that I could reduce the number of moves even further. But then, maybe I can reduce the number of moves in the short-legged case too. How can I really be sure that $f^2 + 2f$ is the best I can do there?

With b boy frogs and g girl frogs, all using the short jumps, I can extend the previous table to include jumps and slides in the following way:

b	2	2	2	3	3	3	4	4	4
g	3	4	5	4	5	6	5	6	7
jumps	6	8	10	12	15	18	20	24	28
slides	5	6	7	7	8	9	9	10	11
N	11	14	17	19	23	27	29	34	39

If our experiments are correct it looks as if the **jumps** are given by

$$j = b.g$$

and the **slides** are

$$s = b + g .$$

That would be consistent with the f a side case I think. And then

$$N = b.g + b + g .$$

Let's see what happens if we put $b = g = f$. Then

$$N = f^2 + f + f = f^2 + 2f.$$

Well, at least the conjectures for j, s and N are consistent. But how can we prove them?

I've had another think about Frogs LS and I've come up with this possibility now. Is this the best possible? How can we ever be sure?

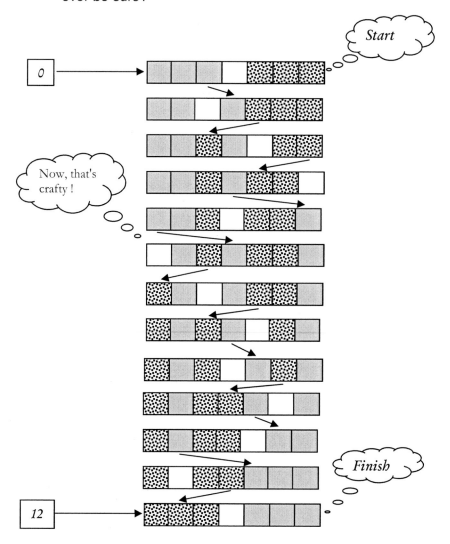

I can't see any system in this one like I could with the short-legged case. But surely if there is a pattern in the number – which I don't have enough evidence to even conjecture – there must be a pattern in the way the moves are made. Surely I don't have to invent the $f = 4$ long-legged case from scratch? It must build from the $f = 3$ case in some way.

And here's another thought. In the swap that involved just 12 moves, a boy frog started first. Could I have done better if I had started with a girl frog? Or, maybe, it just wouldn't have worked at all!

And then that gives me another horrible thought. Maybe there is another problem – Frogs LL. What if I've landed in a reunion of long-legged frogs? What happens if all the frogs have long legs? How many moves are necessary now?

Or, maybe, it isn't possible! It's certainly not possible if only one frog is on either side because the two single frogs can't get past each other. What about two frogs a side? You'll notice that I have a hiccup on the left side before I do it.

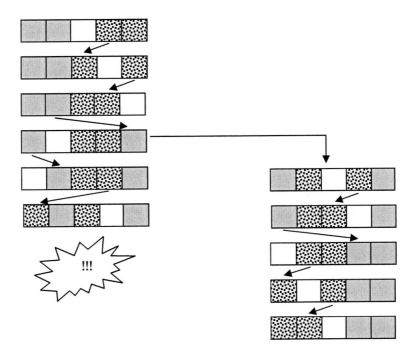

So I did it, but it's faster moving two long-legged frogs with two short-legged frogs. I can do that in five moves! Is that just because the numbers are small and there isn't room to move? Can I do the all-long-legged three-a-side frog jumping competition in fewer moves than the mixed case?

I'm off for another coffee.

From Chapter 9 we have the following remnants.

With f frogs on each side the two frog teams can be swapped in precisely

$$f^2 + 2f$$

moves with f^2 of these being jumps and $2f$ being slides.

With b frogs on one side and g frogs on the other, the two groups' positions can be swapped in

$$bg + b + g$$

moves with bg of these being jumps and $b + g$ being slides.

And the other remnant was

What on earth is happening with long-legged frogs in both Frogs LS and Frogs LL?

I'm still not sure what is happening if we have long-legged frogs and short-legged frogs trying to change sides. However, I'm prepared to give my attempts at best possible numbers and to suggest that I think I know how the case where there are two short-legged frogs and any number of long-legged frogs might go. I'll hold off on the latter for a while. In the meantime, here are some numbers that I hope are best possible, but I really don't guarantee that they are.

Long-legged frogs	Short-legged frogs	Total moves
1	1	3
2	2	5
3	3	11
4	4	20
5	5	30

Let me show you how I got the 11 moves for the $f = 3$ case. (Here the B's are long-legged and I've simplified the representation.)

B	B	B		G	G	G
B	B	B	G	G		G
B	B		G	G	B	G
B	B	G		G	B	G
	B	G	B	G	B	G
G	B		B	G	B	G
G	B	G	B		B	G
G	B	G	B	G	B	
G	B	G		G	B	B
G	B	G	G		B	B
G		G	G	B	B	B
G	G	G		B	B	B

There are two things that worry me. First, I can't see a simple quadratic that would fit the data. And, second, I can move the four frogs a side in at least four different ways, so I can't think how an algorithm might go in general.

▷ In the rest of this chapter, first I want to try to prove Conjecture 1; second I want to let you see how that melds into Conjecture 2; and finally I want to do as much of the long-legged situations as I can. I'm hoping that by seeing that case you'll begin to realise why I need to be so careful over the f a-side situation.

So, some preliminary words about Conjecture 1 and why I'm about to do what I'm about to do. I'll also give a proof of Conjecture 2 and my best attempt at the $l = 4$ case of the Frogs LL problem.

It's tempting to think that after you have done the regular f a-side problem for f up to 5 or even 6, you know everything that is going on and there is no more to do. You start to get into the swing of things and it's clear to you that you could keep going on the same way for any value of f you like to choose. Stop the traffic in the High Street, invite 1,000 male volunteers and 1,000 female volunteers to step out of their cars and sit on 2,000 of 2,001 lily pads and I can tell you how to swap them over. (Or maybe you'd prefer to do it at half-time in the World Cup with $f = 50,000$!) So you have a pretty good idea of an algorithm for swapping frogs, even if you might not be able to write it down precisely.

Even if you could find 2,000 volunteers with the time to engage in the exercise, all that you would have proved is that you can swap them over and that that takes at most 1,002,000 moves. Maybe, though, someone else can do it in 1,001,999 moves. How could you say they were wrong? Well, perhaps I should say, how could you **show** they were wrong?

What I plan to do now is to show that

    (i)   if the frogs can be swapped then there **have** to be f^2 jumps and $2f$ slides. I'm going to use some counting here;

and

    (ii)   that **there is** an algorithm that will swap the frogs in $f^2 + 2f$ moves. I'm going to use Mathematical Induction here.

Let me underline the two steps. First I will show that to get the frogs where they need to go, requires f^2 jumps and $2f$ slides. So that N, the total number of moves, can't be less than $f^2 + 2f$, that is

$$N \geq f^2 + 2f.$$

Then I'll produce an algorithm to show that it can be done in that many moves. Having established both of these, then I'll be sure that

$$N = f^2 + 2f.$$

Now you might think that all I have to do is to prove that (ii) can be done because this shows that the moving can be done in $f^2 + 2f$ moves. But if we only had that, there is the chance that someone else may find an algorithm that would work in fewer moves (see the discussion about two long-legged frogs on page 113). So (i) will make sure that our algorithm in (ii) gives us the best possible result. And I don't know how I can get away with any **shorter** argument than this if I'm to prove Conjecture 1.

I know that Conjecture 2 can be proved in the same way, but I'll leave you to generalise the proof I give of Conjecture 1 at the end of the paragraph.

One final comment, the proof of (i) is relatively easy. However, (ii) is not and will require much more concentration. You may want to skim through it the first time and go back to it later. However, it might be useful for a World Cup half-time entertainment sometime.

▷ To introduce (i), I'll start with $f = 3$. If you go back to the previous chapter you'll see that j, the number of jumps, is 9 and s, the number of slides, is 6. How can we show that we need at least 15 moves then ?

Look at one boy frog and one girl frog. I don't know which one will do the jumping when they meet, but they must be involved in one jump otherwise they can't get past each other. So one boy frog then has to be involved in three jumps as he has to get past three girl frogs. But there are three boy frogs so there have to be $3 \times 3 = 9$ jumps.

In the same way each boy frog in the general f case has to be involved with f jumps, either jumping or being jumped. So altogether there have to be f^2 jumps.

Now about the slides; this is not such a direct argument. Think about the number of lily pads each frog has to cover. In the $f = 3$ case, if a girl frog goes directly to her final position she will have to cross four lily pads. I use the word 'cross' loosely. She may have to actually land on some of these. The number of lily pads used then is 3×4 for the girls and 3×4 for the boys, to give a total of 24 lily pads used.

In the general case this amounts to

$$f(f + 1) + f(f + 1) = 2f^2 + 2f.$$

It should be noted that this number of lily pads has to be crossed even if all frogs don't cross the same number of lily pads. That is, if some frogs go less than $f + 1$ and some go more. To see this note that $1 + 2 + \ldots + f$ lily pads are crossed by the girl frogs in getting to the centre lily pad and the same number is crossed while the girl frogs are getting to their final positions.

OK, but, in the $f = 3$ case, we have nine jumps and nine jumps use 18 lily pads – there are two lily pads used in a jump. So we have

$24 - 18$ lily pads to use up. These can only be used by slides. Since slides only use one lily pad, then we have $24 - 18 = 6$ slides.

The number of moves we **have** to have is $9 + 6 = 15$.

Going back to f frogs-a-side, we see that $2f^2$ lily pads are used by jumps. Hence we have

$$(2f^2 + 2f) - 2f^2$$

lily pads to be used by slides. So there are $2f$ slides. In total this gives a requirement of $f^2 + 2f$ moves.

Now to the algorithm (ii). I'll do this in a series of steps. Before I do though, I should say that this proof of the Theorem is due to Paul Shutler of the National Institute of Education, Singapore.

Before I start I just want to show some notation that will be handy in a minute. For instance,

$$[BB...B \_ GG ... G]$$

stands for

and (I'll explain the lower case letters in a minute)
$$b[BB...B \_ GG...G]g$$
stands for

Lemma: Frogs in the position [BB...B _ GG...G], the starting position, can be moved to the position [_ GBGB...GB] in $\frac{1}{2}f(f+1) + f$ moves.

I'll proceed by Induction.

Step 1: I'll leave you to check that the result is true for $f = 1$.

Step 2: Now assume the result is true for f. That is assume that for f frogs a side, I can move from the position

[BB...B_GG...G] to the position [_GBGB...GB]

in $\frac{1}{2}f(f+1) + f$ moves. Or equivalently, because we might move the girl frogs first, to

[GBGB...GB_]

in the same number of moves.

Step 3: Now consider f B's and G's and an extra boy and girl frog who I shall call b and g, respectively. The initial position for these frogs I'll assume to be

b[BB...B_GG...G]g.

By Step 2, I can move these frogs to

b[GBGB...GB_]g

in $\frac{1}{2}f(f+1) + f$ moves. One further slide gets them to

b[GBGB...GBg] _.

Then if all the B's and b jump over all the G's and g, the frogs get to

_[GbGB...GBg]B

in a further $f + 1$ moves. But this is the final position for the Lemma and has taken a total of

$$\{\tfrac{1}{2}f(f+1) + f\} + 1 + (f+1) = \tfrac{1}{2}(f+1)(f+2) + (f+1)$$

moves. So the result is true for $f + 1$ frogs on each side, and the induction succeeds.

Now we can prove the second result.

> **Theorem:** The frogs can be swapped in $f^2 + 2f$ moves.

 **Proof**   Consider f frogs of each colour, $(f - 1)$ labelled B or G and one pair labelled b and g for clarity.

Now

[B...BBb_gGG...G]   becomes   [_gBGB...Gb]

in $\frac{1}{2}f(f + 1) + f$ moves - by the Lemma.

Next slide the g so that in one move

[_gBGB...Gb] becomes [g_BGB...Gb] = g[_BG...BG]b.

From here move

g[_BG...BG]b to g[GG...G_BB...B]b = [gGG...G_BB...Bb]

in $\frac{1}{2}(f - 1)f + (f - 1)$ moves - by Lemma 1 applied 'reversed' to the $(f - 1)$ frogs enclosed by the square brackets. Hence the total number of moves is

$$\{\tfrac{1}{2}f(f + 1) + f\} + 1 + \{\tfrac{1}{2}(f - 1)f + (f - 1)\} = f^2 + 2f$$

and we are finished.

And now I hope that you can see my difficulty with Frogs LL and Frogs LS. I haven't really been able to establish a working algorithm. So there's no way I'm going to an international airport, 'borrow' 2,000 bored, waiting, and long- or short-legged travellers and line them up on 2,001 seats between Gates 10 and 74 and start to swap them over. Since I don't have a working algorithm for moving the frogs in either long-legged problem, I don't have an upper bound for f frogs a side. This means (i) I don't have a decent conjecture and (ii) I don't have anything on which I can use Mathematical Induction or any other proof technique.

But even worse, I don't have even the simple, counting part, of the problem under my belt. Are there f^2 jumps? Hardly.

Some of the jumps here involve three frogs: One jumper and two jumpees. It wouldn't be so bad if the two jumpees were both short-legged and coming towards the jumper. That might give

$$f(\tfrac{1}{2}f) = \tfrac{1}{2}f^2 \quad \text{jumps.}$$

But you can see in some of the examples that a jumpee is as likely to be long-legged as short-legged.

- So how can you count the number of jumps?
- And how can you deduce the number of slides?

A new idea is needed.

- What ideas do you have?

I'd love to be able to scaffold you here to a conclusion, but as I don't have any idea what that conclusion is it's very difficult for me to help you to go in the right direction. Actually this is the reason that I've taken all of the other problems in this book to what I think is their natural conclusion. If you can see where a problem might end, you can help your students to get there. If you don't know an end, then you are as much in the dark as your students.

But in this Frog LS problem the ideas from the short-legged problem aren't going to hold up. You can't even use the short-legged value from Conjecture 1 to give an upper bound for the long-legged case. It would seem likely that the long-legged problem could be completed in fewer moves than the short-legged one. However, I haven't got any argument to justify this either. So I think that it might be worth experimenting.

Let's try the case of 2 short-legged frogs (S) and ℓ long-legged ones (L). Below I give the example of $\ell = 4$, which shows that the change can be effected in 9 moves. (This compares with 14 if all frogs were short-legged.) In general, the same change for ℓ long-legged frogs seems to require $2\ell + 1$ moves.

- But how can we prove this?

- In particular, how do we know that it can't be done in less?

Start	S	S		L	L	L	L
1		S	S	L	L	L	L
2	L	S	S		L	L	L
3	L		S	S	L	L	L
4	L	L	S	S		L	L
5	L	L		S	S	L	L
6	L	L	L	S	S		L
7	L	L	L		S	S	L
8	L	L	L	L	S	S	
9	L	L	L	L		S	S

However, things are even worse if I change tack slightly again and make both sets of frogs long-legged. First we can't even **do** the $f = 1$ case. We can just never get one such frog past another unless one of them jumps **off** the lily pads. And I think the best that can be done with two long-legged frogs on either side is eight moves. This compares with six moves for two short-legged frogs-a-side. So there is no guarantee that we can either :

    (i) do the f long-legged frogs per side

or   (ii) that if we can it will give us fewer moves than the corresponding short-legged case.

But there is another problem that highlights why we need both steps (i) and (ii) in the proof of the regular Frog Problem. As I did with Frogs LS, take 2 frogs on one side and ℓ on the other. I did this with a class and we came up with this cunning inductive step.

$$[B\ B\ \_\ G\ G\ G]\ \text{moves to}\ [G\ G\ \_\ B\ B\ G]$$

in the 8 steps we noted above;

$$[G\ G\ \_\ B\ B\ G]\ \text{moves to}\ [G\ G\ G\ B\ B\ \_\ ]$$

in the 1 step; and

$$[G\ G\ G\ B\ B\ \_\ ]\ \text{moves to}\ [G\ G\ G\ \_\ B\ B]$$

in 2 more steps.

If $\ell = 4$, we'd get

$$[\text{GGG\_BBG}]$$

by the set of moves for $\ell = 3$. Then the last 3 moves above will get us to

$$[\text{GGGG\_BB}].$$

So from hereon we can apply the last three steps to show that we keep going up in 3 steps as we increase the value of ℓ. This gives us a total number of moves of $3\ell + 2$.

All very fine, until one boy discovered that for $\ell = 4$, he could swap the frogs in 12 moves! So the step (ii) algorithm alone didn't work because we hadn't established that we **had** to have $3\ell + 2$ moves at step (i)!

 Here is a proof by Paul Shutler of the second part of the Frogs Problem where there are a different number of frogs on each side.

Lemma: B[_GBGB...GB] can be changed to [GBGB...GB_]B in g + 1 moves where there are g G-B pairs and an extra boy frog B at the left hand end.

Similarly B[GBGB...GB_] can be changed to [_GBGB...GB]B in g + 1 moves.

Proof: To do this, first slide the left hand B to the right and then each G jumps starting from the left.

Theorem: The frogs can be swapped in bg + b + g moves.

Proof: Treat the case b > g only. The case b < g follows by symmetry.

Consider (b − g) boy frogs next to g boy and g girl frogs,

$$\text{BB...B[BB...B\_GG...G].}$$

This can be changed to

$$BB...B[\_GBGB...GB]$$

in $\frac{1}{2}g(g + 1) + g$ moves by the Lemma in the text.

Now apply the Lemma above $(b - g)$ times to shift the $(b - g)$ B's from left to right. This gives

$$[\_GBGB...GB]BB...B$$

if $(b - g)$ is even or

$$[GBGB...GB\_]BB...B$$

if $(b - g)$ is odd.

Next slide the left hand G (or right hand B) to give

$$G[\_BGBG...BG]B\ BB...B \quad \text{or} \quad G[BGBG...BG\_]B\ BB...B.$$

These become

$$G[GG...G\_BB...B]B\ BB...B$$

in $\frac{1}{2}(g - 1)g + (g - 1)$ moves by the Lemma of the text.

Hence the total moves required are

$$\{\tfrac{1}{2}g(g + 1) + g\} + \{(b - g)(g + 1) + 1\} + \{\tfrac{1}{2}(g - 1)g + (g - 1)\}$$

$$= bg + b + g.$$

 Here is the $\ell = 4$ case of the Frog LL problem.

$$B\ B\ \_\ G\ G\ G\ G$$

$$B\ \_\ B\ G\ G\ G\ G$$

$$B\ G\ B\ G\ \_\ G\ G$$

$$B\ G\ B\ G\ G\ \_\ G$$

B G _ G G B G

B G G _ G B G

_ G G B G B G

G _ G B G B G

G G G B _ B G

G G G _ B B G

G G G G B B _

G G G G B _ B

G G G G _ B B

11 Rolling square problem

Take a 3 x 3 square and a 1 x 1 square. Put the smaller square, (drawn in bold) in the diagram, on the larger one as shown.

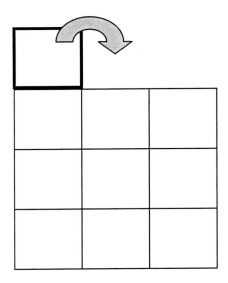

Figure 11.1 The rolling square problem

Now 'roll' the smaller square around the larger one without slipping, so that it is always in touch with the larger square. What is the locus of any one of the vertices of the smaller square as it rolls around the larger square? In other words what is the path drawn out by one of the corners?

As usual there ought to be room here to extend and generalise.

In some ways this isn't a problem but rather an excuse for an investigation that will cover some geometry. The reason that I say this isn't a problem is that it should be clear that the path to a solution is to roll the small square and see what happens. Apart from the pretty shapes that arise here the interest is in the extensions and generalisations. But it is a nice chance to experiment geometrically.

This problem has almost certainly been looked at before but it came out of a professional development course I was sitting in on at the University of Chichester. I guess it was motivated by epicycloids: circles rolling around circles. (You can find these by a web search – some sites have nice animations. They are well worth looking into.) Since then I have used it several times with success. It's interesting that often these sessions start slowly, at least slowly as far as the mathematics is concerned. Students seem to like the task of constructing this locus and the ones you get using $n \times n$ squares for various n. But at first, it just seems a pleasant task that gives some nice shapes. However, when students finally see the loci for a range of values of n their eyes light up and the possibly dull and routine tracing of loci seems to have been really worthwhile.

Let me just talk a little about practical matters for a moment. I find that a small square (the rolling square) of about 5cm by 5cm is good to use. It's just big enough to handle comfortably. You will find that smaller sized squares are a little harder to manipulate. Keeping a pencil attached to one corner as the students roll the square is harder for smaller squares. Actually it's not that easy for any sized square. For this reason I suggest that you trace out the locus for the first time in pencil (and, of course, you will make errors at first so using pencil makes it easier to correct your mistakes). Then, when you can see where the arcs of the various circles should go, you might draw them in using compasses guided by your original pencil marks. This second drawing might be in a colour and slightly thicker than normal pencil. By using compasses you will get a better idea of the exact shapes of the loci and you will certainly appreciate their symmetry more than you will by a rough, hand pencilled drawing.

Of course, if you have access to a computer, you should be able to speed the whole process up and get some very accurate loci. What's more this will give you a whole lot of information in a relatively short time. In fact when I was doing this for the first time with Carol Knights at Chichester, we used an interactive whiteboard. First we saw what the basic shapes were for the different positions of the smaller square (see **Figure 11.1**) and simply copied them into their correct places as we mentally moved the smaller square around the larger one.

A 5 cm square does cause another difficulty though. When you are looking for the loci with larger $n \times n$ squares, you are forced to use a large piece of paper otherwise the locus is likely to try to escape off of the paper. If you are doing the exercise with a class, I would also suggest that you divide the various n among them so that you have at least three of each n. If you are doing it by yourself, I suggest that you spend an hour or so experimenting with n up to 13 or so and then leave the loci and come back later and check what you have done. It would be useful, perhaps to do the $n = 3$ and 4 cases first and then check your results against **Figures 11.2** and **11.3** to see that you are on track.

Now a small warning: you might get more than one locus for each n. In my experience there is a tendency to think that once you have found one locus for a given n, there is nothing more to find. But there may be!

The locus that you should find for the original problem with $n = 3$ is shown in **Figure 11.2**. Here A is the left hand bottom vertex of the small square; A is the point on the square that I have followed to produce the locus in **Figure 11.3**. Rather surprisingly perhaps, the same locus is found, to within a rotation, if any other vertex of the square is considered. The locus is rather pleasant with one axis of symmetry through the top left/bottom right diagonal of the fixed square.

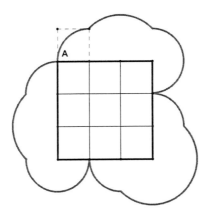

Figure 11.2 The locus of the point A for $n = 3$

Some people like to see things in these loci and even decorate them to give them a personality. This one is popularly known as "the frog" but you have to rotate it a bit to see that with any clarity.

But let's be systematic about this. You should quickly see why the single locus for $n = 1$ is often called Mickey Mouse. The case $n = 2$

is the first occasion that you get more than one locus. You might think of these as two butterflies but one of them is surely a pair of Siamese Mickeys joined at the head. These two loci are also the first we have seen that have more than one axis of symmetry. But I want to show you the $n = 4$ case (**Figure 11.3**).

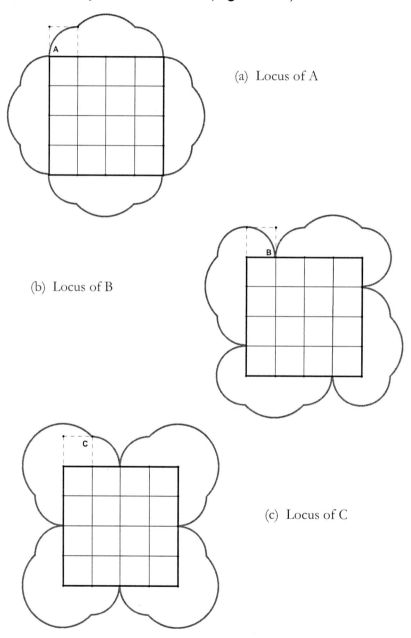

(a) Locus of A

(b) Locus of B

(c) Locus of C

Figure 11.3 The locus of points A, B, and C for $n = 4$

The first question to ask about **Figure 11.3**, is what happened to the point D at the top left hand corner of the small square? Have I forgotten to tell you about this locus or do we already have it?   And what about the symmetry? The loci in **Figures 11.3** (a) and (c) have about as much symmetry as you could expect starting from a square and the locus of **Figure 11.3** (b) has nice rotational symmetry about an axis perpendicular to the 4 x 4 square. That ought to be worth discussing with any class. But so might the question of why some n give only one locus and some give three? And is it possible that we can find an n that gives us *four* different loci?

To get the feel of this general problem you need to get the data. I suggest that you start with $n = 1, 2, 3$ and 4. That should get you moving and get all of your starting up problems sorted. But then it would be good if you could get up to at least $n = 13$. (By then you may well be able to see what is going to happen without actually pencilling around the moving square.) The next stage is a period of looking and comparing. What can you see? What patterns are here? How does one develop onto another?

Write down all that you can see and all of your conjectures. And remember that you are at least thinking about shape, symmetry, number of possible loci for each n, and perimeter. So there's a lot going on. At this point it's a good idea to draw up a **table**. This is a strategy that almost always makes the scattered data that you have, more manageable.

Then let the discussion start! At random I notice that there is something up with the odd numbers. If n is odd, then you get only one locus and the perimeters seem to be going up in a nice orderly manner. Why is that? How can we justify that?

Now I have to say at this point that I can't see how to do that directly. If you have any ideas I'd be more than glad to hear about them. I do think that I can go from $n = 4k + 1$ to $4k + 5$ and from $n = 4k + 3$ to $4k + 7$, though. So with a bit of luck I might be able to put together a proof by Induction working first with $n \equiv 1$ (mod 4) and then with $n \equiv 3$ (mod 4). The only thing that worries me is that proofs by Induction don't really give me any understanding of what's going on. What is it about the odd numbers that forces only one locus, for example? I'd like the proof to give me some insight into this question and Induction just doesn't do that.

What else do we get out of the table? Did you notice the symmetry that we got from $n = 4, 8$ and 12? And there were always **three** loci. What happens between 4 and 8 and 8 and 12? Clouds! We add clouds to the sides. Where? When? Another proof by Induction surely if we look at the loci for $n \equiv 0$ (mod 4)? That only leaves $n \equiv 2$ (mod 4) and I'm sure that you can work things out from here.

And is this (**Figure 11.4**) any use for one more outstanding understanding question?

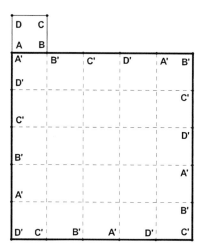

(a) The 5x5 square

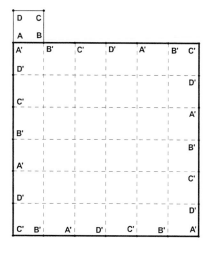

(b) The 6x6 square

Figure 11.4 Helpful diagrams - or another mystery?

That has pretty well cleaned up the Rolling Squares Problem - for fixed squares anyway. But there's no reason why we can't extend or generalise. In fact I hope that you'd be disappointed now if I didn't. It's at this point that I have a confession. Actually when I first contemplated this idea the shape that was fixed was a rectangle. So it looks as if we might now have a generalisation to $m \times n$ rectangles. Something different comes out straight away. Look at the case of the 1×2 rectangle (Figure 4).

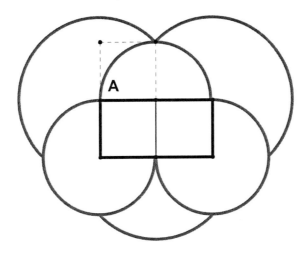

Figure 11.5 The locus for a 1×2 rectangle

So far as the fixed square loci were concerned, once around the square and they closed up. But with the 1×2 rectangle, the rolling square has to go around twice before the locus closes up. For what rectangles does that doubling occur? Can we predict when it will happen? Do we ever have to go round three times to get completion? How much of the locus is covered twice before it is completed? Clearly there's a lot going on here. Can we nail it all?

But why stop at rectangles? Without my sanctioning it, in one of the sessions that I did with this problem one of the students tried to roll an equilateral triangle around a bigger equilateral triangle. When I caught up with him I thought that it was a neat idea but there seemed to be no symmetry in what was a very symmetric situation to begin with. It took me a long time to work out that he had one side of his fixed (equilateral) triangle bigger than the other two!

I suspect that rolling a regular n-gon around a bigger regular n-gon will turn out to be quite interesting. And it should generalise what we did with the squares. In general what takes the place of the clouds? Oh, and why does the bigger n-gon have to have sides that are multiples of the smaller ones?

I guess we should start here with a rectangle because that may enable us to generalise what we did in the previous chapter. After all, a square is a special type of rectangle. However, if you want to go off now and explore equilateral triangles or anything polygonal, regular or otherwise (and what is wrong with circles or ellipses), you should go off right now and see what you come up with.

Now I think that we ought to be a bit systematic about this if we are in it for the long haul. First let's analyse the situations. It seems to me that there are two types of points on the large rectangle about which the small square is rotating. Such points are either interior to a side of a rectangle or on the corners of the rectangle. And the interior points are all multiples of a unit from each corner.

Relative to each of these points there are four positions for the point on the square that are generating the locus. These points are: top left, top right, bottom right, bottom left.

To do this problem it is not necessary that you or your students notice this. It's possible to produce loci for many rectangles just by moving a square around to see what happens overall. However, after some analysis you should be able to generate loci by thought more efficiently than by tracing the movement of one corner of the small square. Of course it is even more efficient if you can program a computer to generate the loci for you. So after you or your students have tried finding the loci of a few rectangles you might scaffold yourself or them to think about analysing what's going on.

Here is my analysis (see **Figure 12.1**) of the eight cases, where *A* is the point being rotated and *X* marks points on the rectangle about which the square is rotating. Recall that the smaller square has side length one.

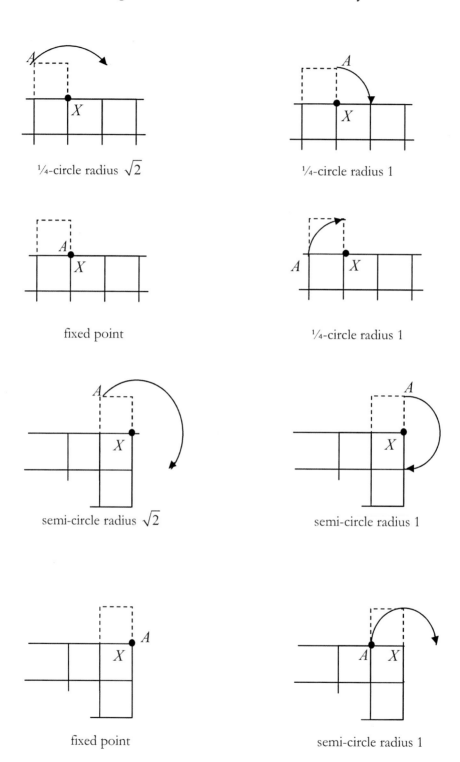

Figure 12.1. The partial loci at different points and positions.

Incidentally, although I've analysed things this way, there is no guarantee that this is the best way. You may well find a better way. So having set things up I'm going to work systematically. What that means to me, at this moment, is that I'll try to find the locus for the $1 \times n$ rectangle, for all n. If that goes well I'll move on to the $2 \times n$ rectangle. Hopefully from there I'll be able to conjecture what happens in the $m \times n$ rectangle. This might lead to a Theorem.

I have presented my **final** list of loci for $1 \times n$ rectangles with $n = 1, 2, \ldots, 7$ in **Figure 12.2**. This was not obtained without errors. It is important to say though, that making mistakes is all part of the problem solving/research process. But getting lost in a foreign city is all part of learning to find your way about, so don't be afraid of getting lost – it's often the beginning of some good learning.

What can I learn from Figure 2? First, it's clear that there are some differences from the $n \times n$ square loci of the previous chapter. There are clearly situations where the small square has to go round the rectangle **twice** in order for the locus to close up. Why is this?

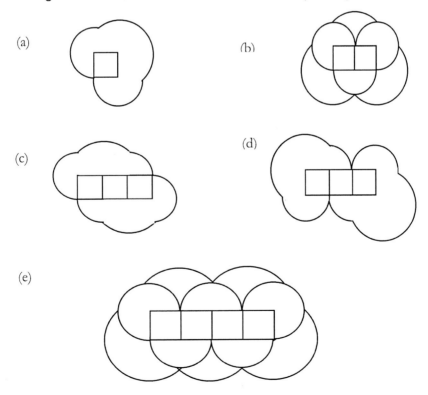

Figure 12.2, Part (i)   The $1 \times 1, 1 \times 2, 1 \times 3$ and 1×4 cases

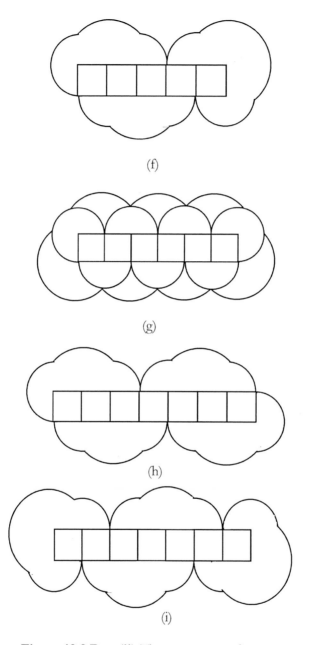

(f)

(g)

(h)

(i)

Figure 12.2 Part (ii) The $1 \times 5, 1 \times 6,$ and 1×7 cases

Second, for some n we get two distinct loci but never more. This is not the same as the square case where we found three loci when the side length was a multiple of four (see **Figure 11.3**). Did we sort out that out in the previous chapter? No, I enigmatically left **Figure 11.4** in the air.

And, third, it looks as if the number that n is congruent to modulo 4 plays an important role. Clearly $n = 2$ and 6 have related loci as do $n = 3$ and 7. With a little imagination, maybe we can see the same thing happening in $n = 1$ and 5 (and maybe we can't!). Or do all of the odds and all of the evens have things in common?

In order to be able to make generalisations, I'll draw up a list - the table below.

n	Number of Loci	Symmetry*
1	1	bilateral about diagonal
2	1	bilateral about centre of rectangle
3	2	both: 180° rotational about centre of rectangle
4	1	bilateral about centre of rectangle
5	1	no symmetry
6	1	bilateral about centre of rectangle
7	2	both: 180° rotational about centre of rectangle

* The axes of symmetry are not precisely defined, but I hope that you can see what I mean in Figure 12.2

Let me see if I can make a successful conjecture. I'll start with the third point above: I should think about the congruence of n modulo 4.

Conjecture 1:   The loci for $n = 4k + i$, $i = 1, 2, 3, 0$, can be obtained from those of $n = 4k - 4 + i$.

Of course this conjecture doesn't tell me how, so I'll look at $n = 2$ and $n = 6$, as well as $n = 3$ and $n = 7$ and see what I can think of. In both cases there seems to be a 1×4 chunk that I can remove from the larger number in order to get the graph of the smaller number. Problematically the two chunks are different. Can I add the same chunk to $n = 6$ as I did to $n = 2$ and get the locus for $n = 10$? Can I add the same chunk to $n = 7$ as I did to $n = 3$ and get the two loci for $n = 11$? Experimentation leads me to believe I can. So does that give me enough ammunition to go from $n = 4$ to $n = 8$?

At this point it seemed to me that the loci for even n might have much more in common than the loci for n modulo 4. Ditto for n odd. The problem with going from one even number to the next is that the two unit chunk that needs to be added in the middle of the next one is always the same BUT it has a different orientation. So, to get over that problem, perhaps I should add the four unit chunk shown in Figure 4 to the middle of $n = 4$. Hopefully that'll give me the correct situation for $n = 8$? (See Figure 5.)

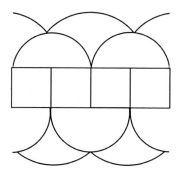

Figure 12.3 A chunk to be added appropriately.

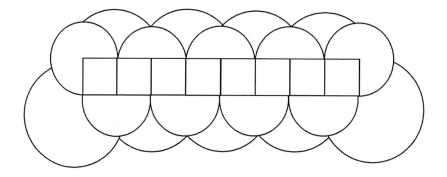

Figure 12.4 A conjecture for the locus of $n = 8$.

Unfortunately I had to turn the chunk upside down to make $n = 8$ work, but when you check through the $n = 8$ case from scratch it works! So there looks like the basis of a theorem here and probably good old Mathematical Induction will get us there. But maybe, given that we are changing the orientation, it might be easier to go from one even number to the next rather than going up in multiples of four.

But if you think there is too much work here before you eventually get to the $m \times n$ case, life is a lot easier if you consider the locus of the **centre** of the small square.

While we're thinking about variations, how about considering what loci are produced when a 2×2 square goes round an $m \times n$ rectangle, or even a $\pi \times \pi$ square around the same quadrilateral?

▷ In the meantime there are a couple of questions we haven't yet answered, but I think are most likely straightforward. These are why do some loci 'close up' on the first time round the $1 \times n$ rectangle and why do some values of n force us to have more than one locus? (I have to say though that working this problem with junior secondary students I have had to do a lot of scaffolding - I had to work really hard to get them to see this. So maybe it's not so obvious after all.)

Clearly, if the little square gets back to its original position in one circuit of the rectangle, the locus will close up. This will certainly happen if the rectangle has perimeter of $4r$ because 4 (the perimeter of the smaller square) goes into $4r$. Now to get that to work, requires $n + 1 + n + 1$ (the magnitude of the perimeter of a $1 \times n$ rectangle) to be divisible by 4. This will happen precisely when n is odd. So do we get 'closure' then, if and only if n is odd?

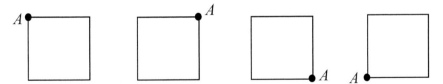

Figure 12.5 The possible positions of A after $2(n + 2)$ rotations.

In **Figure 12.5** we show the four possible positions of A when the square first gets back to its initial position on the rectangle. Only one of these (depending on where you started) produces closure. So we do get the 'if and only if' result. But we also get a bonus. The same reasoning can be used to show that we have closure on the $m \times n$ rectangle if and only if $m + n$ is odd. Just count the number of outer 'units' in the $m \times n$ case. Along the top and bottom there are n and along the sides there are m. So closure results if and only if 4 divides $2(m + n)$. There $m + n$ needs to be even. Ooops! Looks like I made a mistake just now. You need to watch out for these. Of course, as I say in class, "these are deliberate errors!" (And if you believe that …)

The other thing I'd like to know is when there is more than one locus, and how many loci are possible. Could we possibly get four loci - thinking ahead, maybe for some m and n in the $m \times n$ case?

Isn't this going to depend on the corners of the $1 \times n$ rectangle or rather what happens to the little square at each of these corners? **Figure 12.5** shows the four possible starting positions of the square as well as whatever we wanted the diagram for in the first place. If $n = 6$, then from **Figure 12.2 Part (ii),** we see we get only one locus. This is because, after reorienting the rectangle appropriately, we get two of the starting positions on the top left of the rectangle (the first and the third positions in **Figure 12.5**) **and** two of the starting positions on the bottom right (the second and the fourth). Since all four starting positions occur **somewhere**, we get just one locus.

For $n = 5$ again we have only one locus. However, this time each starting position is to be found at a different corner. The positions at the top right and bottom left are 'back to front'. What's happening here is that turning the square anti-clockwise we'd get the same locus. Anti-clockwise rotation fills in the backward starting positions at the top right and bottom left.

I'm sure that you can see what happens for all n in the $1 \times n$ case. Looking at **Figure 12.2** ought to give it away. However, can you predict the $m \times n$ case? There is a long way to go to get here and you might want to go via $m = 2$ and 3. Do we only get one or two loci then? Is it possible to get **four** loci for some m and n? Probably not! But *I* wouldn't trust me. However, you can trust **Figure 11. 4**. That will show you exactly what is going on here.

13   The Fish Problem

The six coins in the diagram on the left (**Figure 13.1**), make up a 'fish' facing to the right. What is the smallest number of coins that need to be moved, so that the 'fish' points to the left?

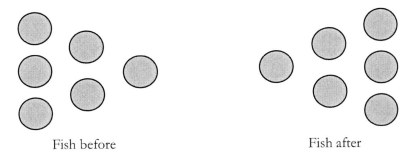

Fish before   Fish after

Figure 13.1 Changing the direction of a fish.

The relative vertical and horizontal positions of the two fish above are irrelevant. The only point of interest here is that the original fish is pointing to the right while the final fish is pointing to the left. It may be that the final fish has been displaced vertically a little.

Generalise, extend, conjecture and prove as much as you can.

▷   There are a number of these 'coin-moving' problems around. I assume that you get to work on the Fish Problem by getting out six coins and simply experimenting. Here's another one that you might like to try.

The Chess Board Problem: Nine coins are placed on the nine squares in a 3 × 3 corner of an 8 × 8 chessboard, see **Figure 13.2**.

A coin can move **only** by jumping over a neighbouring coin onto an empty chessboard square. This jumping can be horizontal, vertical or diagonal in direction. So, for a start, none of the four coins in the corners of the 3 × 3 array can move, but all of the other coins can. In particular, the centre coin has three possible moves: vertically up; diagonally up and horizontally across.

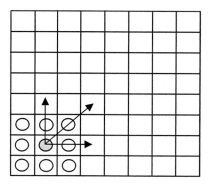

Figure 13.2 The nine coins in their original position
and the possible moves of the central coin.

Here's the problem then. Using only the moves I have defined (no
coin can move unless it has a neighbour with a coin-less square on
the other side), can the group of nine coins be moved to the 3×3
sub square in the top right hand corner of the board or the 3×3
sub square in the bottom right hand corner (see **Figure 13.3**).

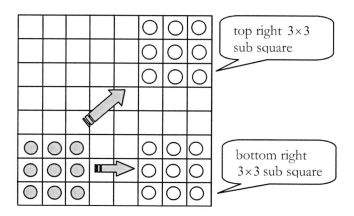

Figure 13.3 Moving the nine coins.

You should see that there is no point asking you about the top left
3×3 sub square because that is exactly the same, by symmetry, as
moving to the bottom right sub square. And if you can move the nine
coins to the bottom right corner, then you can probably repeat the
moves to get the coins to the top corner. On the other hand, if you
can't get the coins to the bottom right corner that tells us nothing
about the move to the top right corner.

Fine, so where do we go from here?

Getting back to the Fish Problem, I assume that you did a little experimentation. You should have quickly seen that you can turn the fish around by moving the right-most three coins over to the left. But I hope that you didn't give up there. You should have then asked, "But can you get away with moving **fewer** than three coins?" Is it possible to get away with moving two coins, or even one? I'll be happy with only a rough argument for the moment. However, I'd like you to have a firm idea of the **minimum** number of coins that you need to move before we go any further. And I'd also like you to have some argument to support your preferred number.

So that inevitably gets us back to the **Chess Board Problem**. How are you going there? I guess one of the first questions is "Can you move the 3×3 array of coins into another 3×3 array somewhere else on the board?" If you can show that this can't be done, then there is nothing more to do. If it can be done, then there are still four possibilities:

- neither corner can be reached;
- both corners can be reached;
- only the bottom right hand corner can be reached;
- only the top right hand corner can be reached.

Which one would you choose and why, especially why?

I guess that it's the Fish Problem's turn now. I think it's possible to move two circles to change the fish's direction. Look at this:

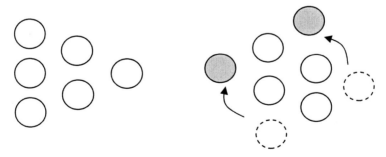

Figure 13.4 Relocating the fish by moving just two coins.

If you relocate the two 'dotted' coins on the left above, as shown by the arrows, the fish turns around. Clearly there is a symmetrical pair of coins on the top sloping side of the fish that will do the same job.

Another pair of coins on the vertical side will actually send the fish moving to the left without changing the horizontal axis of the fish. (The same coins can also divert the fish so that it is moving down diagonally to the right.)

The question is, though, can we change the fish's direction by moving only **one** coin? The difficulty here is maintaining a vertical side of the fish with three coins. Essentially the fish is made up of three columns of coins: the one to the left has three coins; the one in the middle has two coins; and the one on the right has only one. Going backwards, making the 'one' column into a 'three' column requires two coins to be moved so we can forget about that. To make the 'two' column into a 'three' column can be done, but it requires us to move the coin from the 'one' column as the new 'three' column has to be on the right. But if we move the right-most coin we have used one coin and we now have *two* 'three' columns.

So the final 'three' column on the turned fish has to be the initial 'three' column. But this has coins to its right that will need to be moved. It looks pretty sure that we can't get away with moving only one coin. So **two** is the minimum we were looking for.

Now you **know** that that's not going to be the end of the problem. What is next? Well our earlier fish has a bigger brother. He's made up of *ten* coins. What's the smallest number of coins that will turn him around?

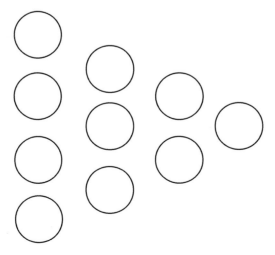

Figure 13.5 The ten-coin fish

The Chess Board Problem is getting a little hard by now. It *is* possible to move the coins from their original 3 × 3 position to another 3 × 3 position, but it's beginning to look as if the relocation I've been able to come up with isn't going to get the group of nine into *any* of the other corners. How about you? Maybe there is another way to move the coins that **will** get them where we want them. Or maybe we can **prove** that we can't get the coins there after all. So we'll either have to fiddle with the moving experimentation until we come up with a process that will do the job, or we'll have to come up with a proof. But proofs can be hard. If there **is** a proof here, can we run it down ?

The fish's bigger brother can be turned in three. Take a coin from each of the corners and add two to the 'two' column and put the third coin out to the left on its own to form the fish's nose.

And, of course, you should now be looking for patterns. What happens if the fish's bigger brother has a bigger sister like the one below?

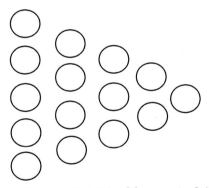

Figure 13.6 The fifteen-coin fish

Is the lady for turning? What is the smallest number of coins that will do the job?

Wait! We didn't show that the bigger brother couldn't be turned using only one or two coins. Can I leave that for you to do? It can get a little messy but it is possible. Think about what I did for the original fish.

It's going to be useful to start a table at this point because you can be sure that I'm not going to stop with the fish's bigger sister. From what I can see so far it might be useful to compare the number of coins that have to be moved, c, with the number of coins, n, in the left-most column of coins that are making up the fish. So far then, we have the table:

n	3	4	5	6	7	8
c	2	3				

Now mathematicians always go for the simplest pattern. It looks so far, then, that c might equal $n - 1$. This is reinforced by looking at the case of $n = 2$ – our original fish's baby sister. She can clearly be turned by moving one coin. That idea comes to grief though with the big sister fish. My feeling is that she needs five coins to be moved to send her in the opposite direction. If so, that would give us the following numbers.

n	2	3	4	5	6	7
c	1	2	3	5		

Now 1, 2, 3, 5 looks like it might be an interesting sequence. In fact, if we put a '1' at the front it would be even more interesting.

$$1, 1, 2, 3, 5,\ldots$$

This is the start of the famous **Fibonacci sequence**. It dates back to 1202 when Fibonacci wrote his book *Liber Abaci*. The whole point of this book was to introduce the decimal system into Europe. The book advocates moving from the Roman numeral system to a place value system, and it does this because of the place value's efficiency with calculation. Have you tried multiplying CCCCLXIII by LXXII using only Roman numerals?

The question is then "Do you get the value of c for some value of n by simply adding the two previous values of c together?" So far

$$1 + 1 = 2, \ 1 + 2 = 3, \ 2 + 3 = 5.$$

The Fibonacci approach would suggest that if we had a fish with a biggest column of $n = 6$, then the number of coins we would need to move to turn it around would be

$$3 + 5 = 8.$$

▷ The Fibonacci sequence has a large number of interesting properties. I suggest you look the sequence up on the web and see what you can find out. There is an interesting connection with the Golden Ratio that might fascinate you.

I don't want to add to the literature on the Fibonacci sequence though. What I do want to do is to point you to the source of all sequences: Neil Sloan's online Encyclopedia of Integer Sequences

htpp://www.research.att.com/~njas/sequences/.

You can while away a happy hour by typing in your favourite sequences and finding out where they came from, who has looked at them before you, and in what connections.

Going to that website and typing in 1, 2, 3, 5, 8, 13 gives you Fibonacci plus *103* other sequences! There seems to be a moral here: six numbers don't give you a unique sequence. In fact, six numbers as a start will give you *any number* of sequences you like!

For a start, you can fit a fifth-degree polynomial in x through six points and then the remaining values of the sequence will come by taking $x = 7, 8, 9, \ldots$ Then you can fit successively higher degree polynomials and get successively more sequences.

Of course, there is a chance that not all the members of these sequences will be integers. But even if you are fussy about sticking to integers, there are lots of sequences to be had. Have a look at these ones:

$$1, 2, 3, 5, 8, 13, 1, 2, 3, 5, 8, 13, 1, 2, 3, 5, 8, 13, \ldots$$

$$1, 2, 3, 5, 8, 13, 2, 4, 6, 10, 16, 26, 2, 4, 6, 10, 16, 26, \ldots$$

$$1, 2, 3, 5, 8, 13, 3, 6, 9, 15, 24, 39, 3, 6, 9, 15, 24, 39, \ldots$$

$$1, 2, 3, 5, 8, 13, 2, 4, 6, 10, 16, 26, 3, 6, 9, 15, 24, 39, \ldots$$

You can almost certainly get an *infinite* number of well-defined sequences that start with 1, 2, 3, 5, 8, 13.

If you think about the Fibonacci sequence and what happens to its *n*th term, maybe you'll see that the fish turning sequence is probably *not* the Fibonacci sequence. Before we do any more experimenting let's see what happens if $n = 10$. By Fibonacci, c would be 55. But the $n = 10$ fish only has 45 coins to start with! Unfortunately the Fibonacci numbers are growing faster than the fish are! Fibonacci is not working here. So where do we go to find c now?

The problem can be resolved by looking more closely at $n = 6$. This next member of the fish school can be turned by moving *seven* (not eight) coins! Take the equilateral triangles formed by three coins on the top left and bottom left corners of the fish and take off the one circle on its nose. **Figure 13.7** shows where to put them.

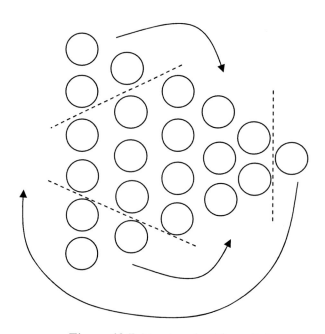

Figure 13.7 Turning the fifteen-fish.

So now our table looks like the one below. For good measure I've added a row labelled s. This contains the total number of coins in any one of our fish. As a bonus I've gone up to what I think is the right answer for $n = 8$. I suggest you go at least as far as 10. And don't forget to try to show the numbers you produce are the **smallest** possible to do the job.

n	2	3	4	5	6	7	8
s	3	6	10	15	21	28	36
c	1	2	3	5	7	9	12

What on earth is the pattern?

 Let's have one more look at the Chess Board Problem. It will only be a brief look in terms of a hint. In **Figure 13.8** below I show a chess board with **shaded** squares – just as you would expect a chessboard to look. This is an important omission from **Figure 13.2**.

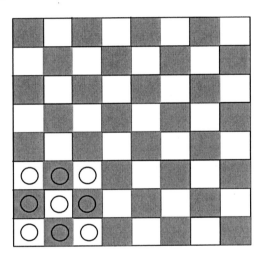

Figure 13.8 The six coins on a *real* chessboard

Does that help at all?

 That's a strange pattern in the last fish table. The number of coins we need to move, c, looks like being a third of the fish's circle,

$$c = \frac{1}{3}s$$

... *nearly.* When s is a multiple of 3 then

$$c = \frac{1}{3}s.$$

But when s isn't a multiple of 3 it's only **nearly** $\frac{1}{3}s$.

For instance, when $s = 10$, $c = 3$ and when $s = 28$, $c = 9$. In fact, the number is always a **part** of $\frac{1}{3}s$, the part remaining when we throw the decimal part away!

Actually there is a function that will do this for you, and it has two names, the **integral part**, or **floor function**. Each use the same symbol $\lfloor \ \rfloor$. So we define $\lfloor x \rfloor$ as follows, for real numbers, x:

$$\lfloor x \rfloor = \text{the biggest integer less than or equal to } x.$$

So $\lfloor 5 \rfloor = 5$, $\lfloor 5.3 \rfloor = 5$ and $\lfloor 5.7842 \rfloor = 5$, Incidentally $\lfloor \pi \rfloor = 3$, where π is the ratio associated with circles.

Looking at this in terms of the fish problem, we notice that

$$\left\lfloor \frac{1}{3} \times 3 \right\rfloor = \lfloor 1 \rfloor = 1; \quad \left\lfloor \frac{1}{3} \times 6 \right\rfloor = \lfloor 2 \rfloor = 2; \quad \left\lfloor \frac{1}{3} \times 10 \right\rfloor = \lfloor 3 \cdot 3333 \cdots \rfloor = 3;$$

$$\left\lfloor \frac{1}{3} \times 15 \right\rfloor = \lfloor 5 \rfloor = 5; \quad \left\lfloor \frac{1}{3} \times 21 \right\rfloor = \lfloor 7 \rfloor = 7; \quad \left\lfloor \frac{1}{3} \times 28 \right\rfloor = \lfloor 9.333... \rfloor = 9;$$

$$\left\lfloor \frac{1}{3} \times 36 \right\rfloor = \lfloor 12 \rfloor = 12.$$ I'm going to suggest a conjecture.

Conjecture: Let s be the number of coins in a fish and let c be the smallest number of coins needed to turn the fish. Then

$$c = \left\lfloor \frac{s}{3} \right\rfloor$$

Can you also see a pattern in the selection of coins to make this turnaround happen? Can you see a pattern in the placement of the coins to effect the turnaround? What else can be done with the Fish Problem?

14 *Finishing off the Fish*

In this chapter I want to prove, if possible, the conjecture of Chapter 13 linking c and $\dfrac{s}{3}$; I want to complete the Chess Board Problem so that I know for sure how that turns out; and I want to think about extending these two problems even further.

Let's go straight to the Fish Problem. How could I demonstrate this link between c and s ? Well, actually, Mathematical Induction might work. It looks as if you could move on from one step to the next. Maybe you could do it in three steps by looking at multiples of 3, multiples of 3 plus 1, and multiples of 3 plus 2. However, I haven't been able to make it work yet so I'm going to pass on the Induction option to you. Let me know how you go.

Now I have seen an argument that uses calculus. But calculus, by its very nature, works with continuous things. After all it was set up to consider continuous motion. I feel uncomfortable with applying continuous variable techniques to discrete objects, although I have to say that sometimes continuous methods have been applied successfully to discrete problems. But the fish problem is a very discrete problem – it deals with whole numbers of coins. So, my inclination here is to try to use discrete techniques. Of course, you might like to work with a function of two variables, maximize it and see what happens.

So then how can I set up the problem and what techniques can I use? First of all I want to visualise the problem by schematically laying the turned fish on top of the original fish (**Figure 14.1**).

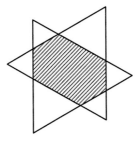

Figure 14.1 The turned fish superimposed on top of the original fish.

Actually the original fish in Figure 1 is in its original position and the turned fish is also in its final position. What I have to do now is to either **minimise** the number of coins that have been moved or **maximise** the number of coins that haven't been moved – those in the common, shaded, area.

Hmmm! When you use words like 'maximise' and 'minimise' you really feel that maybe calculus is where you should be going. Find a function, differentiate, put equal to zero – that's all good calculus stuff that you can use to find maxima or minima. I'll resist the urge to use calculus though.

It's probably important about now to say that the shaded part must have **some** coins in it. After all we could move every coin so that the fish has its direction changed.

Now what I plan to do first is to look at the case where $n = 3a$. The method is exactly the same for $n = 3a + 1$ and $n = 3a + 2$, essentially only the algebra is different.

At this point too, Figure 1 suggests that we might want to know how big the equilateral triangles of coins are that are moved in the $n = 3a$ case.

I have come up with the following conjecture, but you need to check that out for some specific cases. You will also need to see what is probably going on with the $3a + 1$ and $3a + 2$ cases, by experimenting a little more.

 **Conjecture**
Let $n = 3a$. Then if the fish has n coins along its external sides, we can turn the fish in no fewer than

$$\frac{1}{6} n(n + 1) = \frac{1}{2} a(3a + 1)$$

moves. This can be effected by moving equilateral triangles of side length $a - 1$, a and a from suitable corners of the original fish.

If we can show this we will know that

$$c = \left\lfloor \frac{s}{3} \right\rfloor$$

is the smallest number of coins that have to be moved to change the direction of the fish. But how can we prove this?

Now let's see where the left vertex, the nose, of the turned fish can be. For a start, it's probably not **inside** the original position of the fish. If it were (at N_1) we could push the turned fish so that its nose was on the **back** of the original fish (at N_2). In the process we'd **increase** the shaded area. So moving the nose from inside the original fish to on its back will increase the number of coins in the overlap (see Figure 2.)

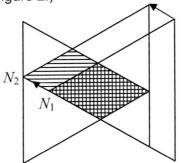

Figure 14.2 Towards a better position of overlap.

Figure 14.2 shows how to move the turned fish parallel to one of the original fish sides so the nose at N_1 is moved to N_2. Note that the horizontally shaded area is clearly bigger than the vertically shaded area. So we can maximise the common area by having no fish nose *inside* the original fish body. So I can assume that I have the situation of **Figure 14.1**, but it's possible that a nose of one fish position is on a side of the other or a tail fin is on a side.

Notice now the final, turned position of the fish in **Figure 14.1**. This will get here no matter **how** we move the coins. However, it's clear that we can get here by moving the coins from the respective small unshaded triangles. So we know that the minimum move **can** be achieved just by using coins in the small equilateral triangle at the corners of the original fish.

What should I do now? Introduce some variables?

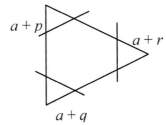

Figure 14.3 Some variables to work with.

In **Figure 14.3** I'm interested in the length of the sides of the triangular pieces that are **not** in the overlap. I'm hoping to find out something about the magnitudes of these. So I've assumed that the top left equilateral triangle has $a + p$ coins along each side, the bottom left one has $a + q$ coins along each side, and the right one has $a + r$ coins on each side.

It may seem perverse to use an a at all, but I hope that will fall out in the wash. Actually the 'a' comes from $n = 3a$ and the p, q and r are just integers – they may be negative. I'm doing this for ease of algebraic manipulation.

In what follows, I'll also need two other variables. Let u be the number of coins that make up the vertical, left, side of the original fish with $a + p$ and $a + q$; and let v be the number of coins so far unaccounted for on the side of that fish that is sloping down. See Figure 4.

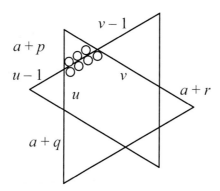

Figure 14.4 Showing how the number of coins changes as well as u and v.

But first I want to notice that $n = (a + p) + (a + q) + (a + r) + 1$. To see this, **Figure 14.4** tells me straight away that

$$n = (a + p) + u + (a + q) \qquad \textbf{(1)}$$
and
$$n = (a + p) + v + (a + r) \qquad \textbf{(2)}$$

In that figure remember that there are coins along the sides of the fish. What's more, there is one more coin on the **inside** edge of the area common to both fish than there is on the outside triangle that we are going to consider soon. So the triangle coming off the part with u coins has only $u - 1$ coins on each side of the part removed. You can check this by doing a specific case with coins.

Now it should be clear by going along a sloping side of the turned fish that

$$n = (u - 1) + (a + p + 1) + (v - 1)$$

$\therefore$ $\qquad n = (u + v) + (a + p) - 1 \qquad\qquad (3)$

From **(1)** and **(2)**

$$u + v = 2n - 4a - 2p - q - r.$$

Substituting in **(3)** we get

$$n = (2n - 4a - 2p - q - r) + a + p - 1$$

$\therefore$ $\qquad n = 4a + 2p + q + r - a - p + 1$

$$= 3a + p + q + r + 1$$

$$= (a + p) + (a + q) + (a + r) + 1 \qquad (4)$$

In what follows I'm going to skip a lot of the algebra. I'll leave it to you to see that there are no errors. You might even check all this using a CAS (Computer Algebra System) calculator.

Remember $n = 3a$. Then $\dfrac{1}{3}\dfrac{n(n+1)}{2} = \dfrac{a(3a+1)}{2}$.

What I'm going to do now is to add the number of coins of the three small triangles and then subtract what I hope is going to be c. My aim then is to show that this difference is never negative. In which case I can never get a smaller value than c to turn the fish around.

OK. So, since the number of coins in one of the equilateral triangles is $\dfrac{w(w+1)}{2}$, where w is the number of coins along one side, the number of coins in the three small triangles is

$$A = \tfrac{1}{2}(a + p)(a + p + 1) + \tfrac{1}{2}(a + q)(a + q + 1) + \tfrac{1}{2}(a + r)(a + r + 1),$$

Then, using **(4)**

$$2A = (a + p)(a + p + 1) + (a + q)(a + q + 1) +$$
$$+ (3a - 2a - p - q - 1)(3a - 2a - p - q)$$

With a little bit of work, this expression simplifies to

$$2A = (a+p)^2 + (a+q)^2 + (a+p) + (a+q) +$$
$$+ (a-p-q)^2 - (a-p-q)$$

Now we hope we can show that A is never less than $c = \dfrac{a(3a+1)}{2}$.

So I'll subtract $2c$ from $2A$ and try to show that this difference is never negative.

$$2(A-c) = \ldots$$

The process of reducing this incomplete equation is a big step, but worth doing. It reduces to

$$2(A-c) = (p+1)^2 + (q+1)^2 + (p+q)^2 - 2.$$

Isn't that pretty!

But it shouldn't be too hard to show that this last expression is never negative.

If $p+1 > 1$ or $p+1 < -1$, $(p+1)^2 > 2$

and we're done since

$$(q+1)^2 + (p+q)^2$$

are always positive. The same thing happens if

$q+1 > 1$ or $q+1 < -1$.

What are we left with? Surely $p+1 = 1$, $p+1 = 0$ or $p+1 = -1$. Likewise $q+1 = 1$, $q+1 = 0$ or $q+1 = -1$.

Let's deal with these in a table. Below I have put the value of $2(A-c)$ in the body of the table for the given values of p and q.

q p	0	−1	−2
0	0	0	4
−1	0	2	8
−2	4	8	16

Does that get us there? Doesn't that prove our Conjecture?

Let's take a breather and think about the Chess Board Problem for a minute of two. Recall the chessboard from Chapter 13.

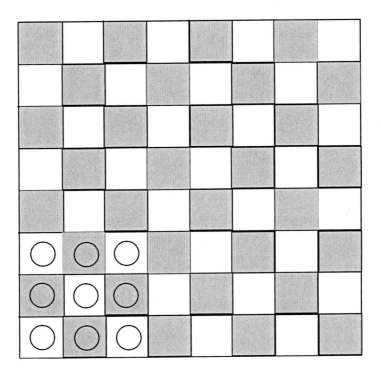

Figure 14.5 The chess board with all squares shaded and the coins in their original positions.

Think about the moves that the coins can make. Because they are all jumping over another coin, they must land on a square that is the same **colour** as the one they are leaving. Just four of the coins start on black squares. But the 3×3 sub-square in the bottom right-hand corner has **five** black squares! So the coins can't go there! What about the top right-hand 3×3 corner?

 Before I say any more about that, I just want you to be sure that you can move the nine coins from a 3×3 array to another 3×3 array. So here is one way it can be done (**Figure 14.6**).

There may be others, of course. But just follow the moves below.

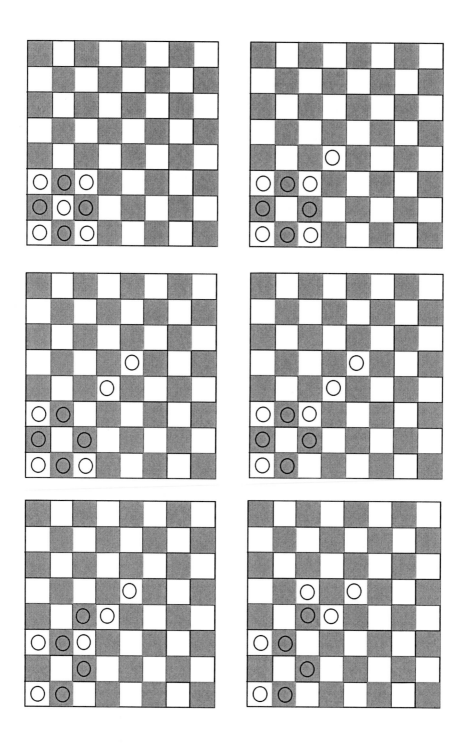

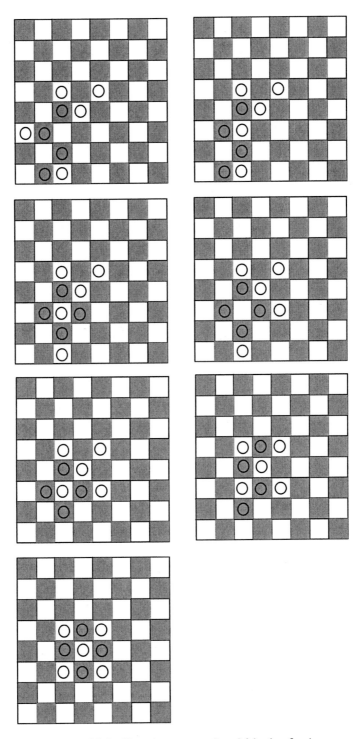

Figure 14.6   How to move a 3 × 3 block of coins.

You have to ask then "So why do that?" How did that help? Can we get the coins to both corners after all?

 Getting back to the Fish Problem, the arguments for Cases 2 and 3 are much the same as for Case 1. There are slight changes in details, but, essentially, you just follow the same route.

But then you have to ask "What have we really achieved?" Well, we've shown that if you want to maximise the area in common between a right and a left facing fish we can do that by making sure that

$$\frac{1}{6}n(n+1)$$

coins are contained in the non-overlapping triangles of each fish.

What's more, we get the minimum when $2(A - c) = 0$. And when does this happen? When

$$p = q = 0 \quad \text{or} \quad p = 0,\ q = -1 \quad \text{or} \quad p = -1,\ q = 0.$$

This, of course, has played straight into the hands of the Conjecture! Time to think.

It's OK isn't it? I *did* prove that the minimum number of coins you need to move is

$$\left\lfloor \frac{n(n+1)}{3} \right\rfloor ,$$

didn't I? And you've now checked that this is also true for

$$n = 3a + 1 \ \text{and}\ 3a + 2$$

haven't you? !

 We still haven't settled the Chess Board Problem as far as the upper right-hand corner is concerned. There the pattern of black squares is the same as the pattern in the bottom left corner where the coins started from. However, the combination of moves in Figure 6 won't move the coins where we want them to go.

So look at the coin in column 1 of **Figure 14.7** that is on a black square.

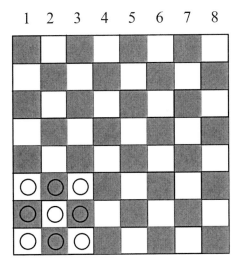

1 2 3 4 5 6 7 8

Figure 14.7 Numbering the columns of the chess board.

When this coin moves it can reach another square in column 1 or a square in column 3. Progressively it can then get to a square in columns 1, 3 or 5, but it can't get to a square in columns 2 or 4. Continuing in this way a coin from column 1 can't get to a black square in column 6 or column 8 where the colour pattern of the squares needs it to go.

So it looks as if neither of the desired relocations can be effected.

Is that all for this problem?

 Well, of course, we are never done, in either of these problems or maybe any other problem for that matter. However it's not easy to see where they might be pushed.

With the Fish Problem we should say that the proof of the Conjecture actually tells us what sized equilateral triangles we need to relocate in each case. The proof also tells us to put the equilateral triangles of coins directly opposite their original positions on the unmoved fish's shape.

As for generalisations, though, what are the other possibilities? It doesn't seem to make sense to think of square fish. How about pentangular ones? Is that very interesting? You could go into three dimensions and have pyramids made of spheres. Can you make a pyramid point another way?

And then the Chess Board Problem. You can probably see that you could 'corner' the coins if you had a 9×9 board or probably any odd by odd board.

Is it of any interest to see for what a, b, m, n you can move an $a \times b$ array of coins from one corner of an $m \times n$ board to any other corner? Maybe that is worth looking at, but I can't see any new ideas coming out of it at the moment. Perhaps you can prove me wrong.

15   Some Powers of 2

The Consecutive Numbers Problem: Note that

$$9 = 2 + 3 + 4 = 4 + 5.$$

In other words, 9 can be written as the sum of consecutive positive integers in two ways. What positive integers **cannot** be written as the sum of two or more consecutive positive integers? Generalise, extend and justify. By now you should immediately and automatically go into experimental mode. I'll be waiting here for you when you get back.

▷ One thing we are almost certainly going to need in this chapter or the next is a way to add up consecutive numbers. Is there a quick way to add up the first ten whole numbers? Is there a quick way to add up the first 100 whole numbers or even the first n whole numbers. If you don't know how to do this, here is another break to let you make some progress.

▷ I'll add 1 to 10 by using circles and crosses in two ways. First, look at the figure below. On the right what you see is the numbers 1 to 10 increasing and coded by circles; on the left you also should see the numbers 10 to 1 going down, depicted by crosses.

10	×	×	×	×	×	×	×	×	×	×	o	1
9	×	×	×	×	×	×	×	×	×	o	o	2
8	×	×	×	×	×	×	×	×	o	o	o	3
7	×	×	×	×	×	×	×	o	o	o	o	4
6	×	×	×	×	×	×	o	o	o	o	o	5
5	×	×	×	×	×	o	o	o	o	o	o	6
4	×	×	×	×	o	o	o	o	o	o	o	7
3	×	×	×	o	o	o	o	o	o	o	o	8
2	×	×	o	o	o	o	o	o	o	o	o	9
1	×	o	o	o	o	o	o	o	o	o	o	10

Figure 15.1 Representing a sum in terms of circles and crosses.

So if you add the number of circles and crosses you'll actually get twice the sum from 1 to 10. Now focus on the inner 11 columns of **Figure 15.1**. This array is a rectangle. This rectangle has 10 rows and 11 columns. So the total number of objects (circles or crosses) it contains is 10×11. That must mean that

$$2(1 + 2 + 3 + 4 + 5 + 6 + 7 + 8 + 9 + 10) = 10 \times 11$$

or　　　$$1 + 2 + 3 + 4 + 5 + 6 + 7 + 8 + 9 + 10 = \frac{10 \times 11}{2} = 55.$$

I'm sure that you can see, using the same argument, that

$$1 + 2 + \ldots + n = \frac{n(n+1)}{2},$$

where I put dots in the middle because it's not possible to put in every number from 3 right up to n.

OK? Then from here it's not difficult to find the sum of any string of consecutive numbers. After all,

$$13 + 14 + 15 + \ldots + 87 = (1 + 2 + 3 + \ldots + 87)$$
$$- (1 + 2 + 3 + \ldots + 12)$$
$$= \frac{87 \times 88}{2} - \frac{12 \times 13}{2} = \frac{1}{2}(7500),$$
$$= \frac{1}{2}(100 \times 75).$$

Where did the 100 come from? What about the 75? Is it possible to generalise this to **any** string of consecutive numbers?

 Just to break your concentration even more but mainly to give you time to answer the last three questions and to overload you with things to do, here is another problem.

The Flight Map Problem:　Air New Britain (ANB) flies to 253 destinations. In its flight magazine there is a map showing these destinations. In the flight map a line joins any two destinations that are linked by an ANB flight. How many different maps are possible? (Allow even the absurd map where none of the 253 destinations is linked by a flight.)

And don't forget to extend, generalise and prove.

I expect your problem solving skills will have come to the fore here. You are unlikely to have generated all of ANB's flight maps, but you probably had the sense to use a good problem solving skill – try a **smaller** case. This might be followed by more smaller cases to try to find a pattern. A table might help you to see a pattern. I hope you did something similar with the Consecutive Numbers Problem. Please do not read on until you have enough data from which you might form some conjectures.

The strange thing about $13 + 14 + 15 + \ldots + 87$

is that it equals $\frac{1}{2}(100 \times 75)$ and $100 = 87 + 13$ while

$75 = 87 - 12$. In general,

$$m + (m + 1) + (m + 2) + \ldots + n = \frac{1}{2}(n + m)(n - m + 1)$$

You might see this, and remember it, by noting that:

- $n + m$ is the **sum of the first and the last terms**
- $n - m + 1$ is the **number of terms** in the sum.

In other words
$m + (m + 1) + (m + 2) + \ldots + n$

$$= \frac{1}{2}(\textbf{sum of first and last}) \times (\textbf{number of terms}).$$

We can easily check this out with a few examples:

- $2 + 3 + 4 = \frac{1}{2}[(2 + 4) \times 3] = 9$

- $\qquad 4 + 5 = \frac{1}{2}[(4 + 5) \times 2] = 9.$

Which gets us back to the Consecutive Numbers Problem. And I'm assuming that you've tried lots of cases – enough to have already produced something like the table below, where a tick ($\sqrt{}$) indicates that the particular number n **can** be written as the sum of some consecutive numbers and a blank indicates that it can't.

n	1	2	3	4	5	6	7	8	9
can			$\sqrt{}$		$\sqrt{}$	$\sqrt{}$	$\sqrt{}$		$\sqrt{}$
n	10	11	12	13	14	15	16	17	18
can	$\sqrt{}$	$\sqrt{}$	$\sqrt{}$	$\sqrt{}$	$\sqrt{}$	$\sqrt{}$		$\sqrt{}$	$\sqrt{}$

What do you think? How do you feel about powers of 2 not being susceptible to a breakdown as the sum of consecutive numbers?

You might worry about the position of 1 here, though. Maybe it's just a small number. On the other hand, maybe we should think of 1 as 2^0, or is that cheating?

Anyway it'll give us a conjecture to get started with. But I'll make a definition first to make our lives easier. Let me call a number **bad** if it can't be written as the sum of a string of consecutive numbers. Then I'll guess this:

 **Conjecture:** n is bad if and only if n is a power of 2.

Notice that I've gone a lot further here than I needed to. I could have just tried "if n is a power of 2, then n is bad" or "if n is bad it's a power of 2". But instead I reached for the sky, put the two together and guessed that both implications are true.

Actually this gives me what is called a **characterisation**. This is essentially an equivalence between two objects. Here, if the conjecture is true, 'bad' and 'powers of 2' are equivalent. Being 'bad' forces n to be a power of 2 and being a power of 2 forces n to be bad. If the Conjecture is true there is no difference in this context between 'bad' and 'powers of 2'.

The reason that mathematicians like characterisations is that it makes life simpler. If the Conjecture is true and we want to know if a number is bad or not, we can simply test to see whether it's a power of 2 or not. The alternative, to see whether n can be written as the sum of some consecutive integers, is a lot more work. (I have mentioned this already in Chapter 4, page 47 where I talked about equivalence.)

Before I have the strength to prove the Conjecture I think I want to get more evidence. Clearly 19 is not a power of 2, but can I prove easily that it isn't bad either. What does your experience with other numbers suggest you might do here? What about your experience with other odd numbers?

$$19 = 9 + 10$$

So 19 isn't bad at all.

But isn't **any** odd number not bad? I'll write any odd number as $2u + 1$, for some whole number u, and leave you to do the rest. No odd number is bad. Well that's some progress I guess. On the other hand, how could we possibly show that any power of 2 is bad? It looks as if the best way to do this might be to use a **Proof by Contradiction** - see Chapter 1, Page 16.

The idea behind a Proof by Contradiction is to assume the opposite of what you are trying to prove and then come up with a contradiction. Because our hypothesis has managed to prove something that can't be true, the original hypothesis was false. Hence we've proved what we wanted to prove.

Let's go back to Chapter 1 for a moment. There we looked at the 4000 Problem. This consists of two sums:

$$
\begin{array}{ccccc}
 & 4 & 0 & 0 & 0 \\
- & a & b & c & 4 \\
\hline
\end{array}
\qquad
\begin{array}{ccccc}
 & 4 & a & b & c \\
- & 4 & 0 & 0 & 0 \\
\hline
\end{array}
$$

What values of a, b, c make the answers to these two subtractions the same? If you remember, we assumed that there **were** digits a, b, c that made the answers the same. Using the standard algorithm for subtracting two 4-digit numbers we found that

$$a = 6, \ b = 3 \ \text{and} \ c = 6.$$

Now if you put these numbers into the two subtraction sums, you get

$$
\begin{array}{r}
4\,0\,0\,0 \\
-\,6\,3\,6\,4 \\
\hline
-\,2\,6\,3\,6
\end{array}
\qquad\qquad
\begin{array}{r}
4\,6\,3\,6 \\
-\,4\,0\,0\,0 \\
\hline
6\,3\,6
\end{array}
$$

Having assumed that values for $a, b,$ and c existed we contradict the fact that the two sums were equal. So there can't be values of $a, b,$ and c for which the subtraction sums are equal.

Somehow, then, I want to show that powers of 2 are bad by assuming that they are not bad and getting some sort of contradiction.

Actually, a classical use of this proof technique goes back to Euclid. Here's how he proved that there are an infinite number of primes.

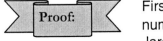 **Proof:** First, suppose there are only k, a finite number, of primes (k might be extremely large, but we'd eventually be able to count up to it). Fine, so the primes can all be listed in increasing order:

Now consider the number
$$p_1, p_2, p_3, \ldots, p_k.$$

$$M = p_1\, p_2\, p_3 \ldots p_k + 1.$$

This is the product of all known primes plus one. Think about M. Is it a prime? No because it's bigger than the assumed largest prime p_k and we have assumed that there is no prime bigger than p_k. Fine, so if M is not prime it must be composite. This means that M must be the product of prime numbers, where possibly some of these primes are repeated.

But we only have primes $p_1, p_2, p_3, \ldots, p_k$ and none of these divides M. So M must be divisible by a prime **other** than $p_1, p_2, p_3, \ldots, p_k$. But this contradicts our original assumption that these were the only primes. Our assumption then was false. So there are an infinite number of primes.

▷ Let's hold the proof that powers of 2 are bad till later on and go back to the Flight Map Problem. How are you going on with it? Did you look at all flight maps with 1, 2, 3, 4, or even 5, destinations? If you didn't, do it now.

If you did, you would have noticed that all of these flight maps have a destination marked by a labelled dot (the label is the name of the destination). What's more a dot is never joined to itself.

Furthermore, there is at most one line between two dots. And finally it doesn't really matter where you put the dots or how you draw the lines you still get the same flight map. (Does that remind you of the London Underground map?)

Oh and you probably have realised that the labels are important. For example, the two flight maps below are quite different because of the places they show flights to.

Figure 15.2 Two different flight maps with four destinations

Did you get anything like the following table for the number of flight maps F with d destinations or dots?

d	1	2	3	4	5
F	1	2	8		

What do you guess the value of F will be for $d = 4$ or $d = 5$? Are there too many flight maps with just four destinations to be able to write them down systematically? If so, what should we do? It might be useful to write out the $d = 1, 2, 3$ cases (see the figure below).

d	Possible maps involving...					Total no. of maps f
	0 flights	1 flight	2 flights	3 flights	4 flights . . .	
1	• A No of ways 1					1
2	• • A B No of ways 1	•—• A B No of ways 1				2
3	(see figure) No of ways 1	(see figure) No of ways 3	(see figure) No of ways 3	(see figure) No of ways 1		8

Figure 15.3 A start on a systematic approach to the Flight Map Problem

Is there some general way that we can work out the number of flight maps with four dots, that have no lines, one line, two lines, three lines, … Oh! How many lines can we possibly have with $d = 4$?

 I know this isn't the right time to move onto another problem but it occurred to me that it might be worth investigating

161

special not bad numbers. Can I say that a number is **good** if it can be written as a string of consecutive numbers in only one way? (Do you see how this opens up further exploration? I'm sure to want to look at **r-good** numbers next when I get stuck on a proof.)

What numbers are good? Is the table below correct?

N	1	2	3	4	5	6	7	8	9
good			√		√	√	√		
N	10	11	12	13	14	15	16	17	18
good	√	√		√	√			√	√

It's hard to see any conjectures here at the moment, so moving off in this direction hasn't helped much. Hmmm! Something weird's going on here:

- certainly all primes seem to be good so far;
- but how did 6 and 14 sneak in while 9, 12 and 15 sneaked out?
- Are all multiples of 3 not good? Then what about 9?

Let's have a rest before the next chapter!

In Chapter 15 I left the Flight Map Problem up in the air. I wasn't able to solve the Consecutive Numbers Problem either; I only managed to get one decent conjecture (on bad numbers and powers of 2); and I seemed to be a long way from solving that. I'll do my best to make progress here, but my guess is that some things will still be left open for you at the end of the chapter.

I'm going to start on the Flight Map Problem because I have at least an idea how that might come out. I'll first show you another table of values that extends the one from the last chapter.

d	1	2	3	4	5
F	1	2	8	64	1024

It doesn't seem hard to me to think of the powers of 2 again in this problem The question is though, "What powers of 2?" Well ...
- from $d = 1$ to 2 we multiply by 2;
- from 2 to 3 by $4 = 2^2$;
- from 3 to 4 by $8 = 2^3$;
- and from 4 to 5 by $16 = 2^4$.

It looks as if:
- in going from $d = n$ to $n + 1$ we multiply by 2^n.

So (i) why and (ii) what is F as a function of n? The last question is easier than the first so I'll go for (ii) and leave you to think about (i).

I want to recall that when we looked at the number of flight maps in Figure 3 in Chapter 15 we found the pattern where the first entry in each row is the number of flight maps with no lines; the second entry is the number of flight maps with one line; the third entry – two lines; the fourth entry – three lines. I assume we can organise the numbers like this for any value of d and for any number of lines.

```
1
1    1
1    2    1
1    3    3    1
```

But doesn't that remind you of something? Where have you seen those numbers before? **Pascal's Triangle** which starts like this

This pattern goes on for ever. To get the next row we just put a 1 at each end and fill up the remaining places by adding together the two numbers immediately above it. Therefore the next row is

1, then $1 + 7 = 8$, then $7 + 21 = 28$, then $21 + 35 = 56$, then $35 + 35 = 70$, and $35 + 21 = 56 \cdots$ etc.

So do we get the flight maps with $d = 4$ by adding 1, 4, 6, 4 and 1? That gives us 16. Hmmm! Not enough. It **is** a power of 2 though.

Actually, if the $d = 4$ case does come from Pascal, the only row that will work is the one starting

       1   6   15 ....

because $1 + 6 + 15 + 20 + 15 + 6 + 1 = 64$. Why don't you see if you can show that these numbers are correct to put in our flight map table below?

1						
1	1					
1	2	1				
1	3	3	1			
1	6	15	20	15	6	1

There are two things to notice here. First Pascal's Triangle gives us the coefficients of the expansion of $(x + 1)^n$, where n links to the row starting

$$1, \quad n, \quad \frac{1}{2}n(n-1), \quad \dots \; .$$

So if you want to add those coefficients in that row you just put $x = 1$. And what we find is $(1 + 1)^n = 2^n$. So every row of Pascal's Triangle adds to a power of 2! That's looking interesting. But which row do we need for the Flight Map Problem? Where do the numbers 1, 2, 3, 6 come from?

Hang on, they are the numbers in the "number of flight maps with 1 line" column. So these numbers are the number of lines in a flight map! How many lines has a flight map with d dots? How can we work that out?

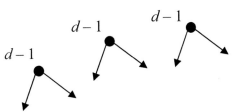

Figure 16.1   The number of possible flights with d destinations
from a given destination

In **Figure 16.1**, every dot can be joined to $d - 1$ other dots, so $d - 1$ lines come out of each dot. There are d dots so there are
$$d(d - 1)$$
lines altogether. But I've counted each line twice, once as it goes into a destination and once as it comes out. So the number of lines

is $\frac{1}{2}d(d-1)$.

Does that work for $d = 1, 2, 3, 4, 5$? Does that mean that

$$F = 2^{\frac{1}{2}d(d-1)} \quad ?$$

Check it out.

If it's true it's kind of nice. However, I think I can get a proof of the F formula **without** using algebraic manipulation or even Pascal's Triangle.

 At this crucial point, of course, I want to go back to the Conjecture of the previous chapter on bad numbers – numbers that are **not** the sum of consecutive numbers. Recall the Conjecture below.

Conjecture: n is a bad number if and only if n is a power of 2.

Recall too that odd numbers, apart from 1 which is after all a power of 2, aren't bad because any odd number can be written as
$$2n + 1 = n + (n + 1).$$
So how can we deal with even numbers that are not powers of 2?

First I want to look at a specific example, 20. Let's assume that 20 isn't bad and then actually find a consecutive string that works. If the consecutive string starts with m and ends with n, we know already, from the last chapter, that

$$m + (m + 1) + (m + 2) + \dots + n = \frac{1}{2}(n + m)(n - m + 1).$$

So
$$\frac{1}{2}(n + m)(n - m + 1) = 20$$

or
$$(n + m)(n - m + 1) = 40.$$

Take a guess here. $40 = 8 \times 5$, so let $n + m = 8$ and $n - m + 1 = 5$. We get two simultaneous equations

$$n + m = 8 \qquad \textbf{(1)}$$
$$n - m = 4 \qquad \textbf{(2)}$$

Solving **(1)** and **(2)** we get $n = 6$ and $m = 2$. Hence
$$2 + 3 + 4 + 5 + 6 = 20.$$

Actually, this is not all plain sailing. If we had taken the factors of 40 to be 10 and 4 we would have found

$$n + m = 10 \qquad \textbf{(1a)}$$
$$n - m = 3 \qquad \textbf{(2a)}$$

It turns out that there are no integer solutions for this. So there is no consecutive string that corresponds to this factorisation of 40. You have to take one even factor and one odd factor to get a consecutive string from the factorisation.

Actually, there is the key! It's also worth noting that the only odd factor of 40 is 5, so in fact we have just shown 20 to be **good** !

You might like to experiment now with a number of numbers to find the consecutive strings of numbers that produce them. Try a few powers of 2 in this mathematical play. In the meantime I want to go back to flight maps.

I think we are now in a position to make the whole Flight Map Problem come out. But I have to do some subtle coding first. What I'm going to do is to change every flight map to a set of brackets with 0s and 1s in them. I'll take the $d = 3$ case to illustrate what I have in mind.

First the coding. I'm going to encode the flight map using the following method:

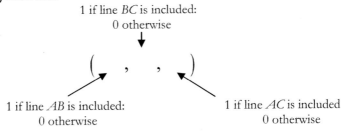

Figure 16.2 Coding for flight maps.

So in front of the first comma I'll put 0 if the line *AB* is in the flight map and 0 otherwise. The second space will mark the presence or absence of the line *BC*; and the third space is for the line *AC*. Here's how that goes in practice.

Flight map	(AB,BC,AC)
A ● B ● ●C	(0,0,0)
A ●\ ●C B ●	(0,0,1)
A ●\ B ●——C	(0,1,1)
A ● B ● ●C	(1,0,1)

Figure 16.3. Encoding some flight maps

I hope you can see that every map has a code and every code produces a map. There is a one-to-one correspondence between maps and codes. Make sure you are convinced. What map is $(1, 0, 1)$?

But this encoding will work for all d. We know now that for a flight map on d dots we have

$$\frac{1}{2}d(d-1)$$

spaces to fill. So once we have given some arbitrary order to the lines, we get set up like this:

$$\underbrace{\begin{pmatrix} AB & AC & \dots & \dots \\ , & , & , & \dots \end{pmatrix}}_{\frac{1}{2}d(d-1) \text{ spaces}}$$

We now have this code for all the flight maps on d dots. How many are there? Thinking of $d = 3$ for a minute, we have two choices for the first space, two for the second and two for the third. Altogether that's

$$2 \times 2 \times 2 = 2^3 = 8$$

just what we want!

In general then, there are 2 choices for the first space; 2 for the second; 2 for the third; ...; and 2 for the $\frac{1}{2}d(d-1)$ th. That's

$$\underbrace{2 \times 2 \times 2 \times \dots \times 2}_{\frac{1}{2}d(d-1) \text{ spaces}} = 2^{\frac{1}{2}d(d-1)}$$

We've done it and hardly **any** algebra in sight!

▷ Now we have to show what powers of two are **bad**. In general to do this requires algebra, but I will start with an example. I'll start with 32, but let me remind you of the similarity of this with 20 on page 166.

Now

$$\frac{1}{2}(n+m)(n-m+1) = 32.$$

So

$$(n+m)(n-m+1) = 64.$$

There are just two possibilities here because 64 is a power of 2. Either it factorises to 1 and 64 (or 64 and 1) or it has two factors that are powers of 2.

Let's suppose they are both powers of 2. In fact we only have to worry about them being even. So

$$n + m$$

is even and

$$n - m + 1$$

is even. From the first of these we know that n and m are both even or both odd. If they are both even, $n - m$ is even and $n - m + 1$ is odd – a pity! If they are both odd, $n - m$ is even and $n - m + 1$ is odd – again a pity! There is no way that $n + m$ and $n - m + 1$ can **both** be even (let alone be powers of 2).

This means we have to fall back to our second option, where it turns out that one of $n + m$ and $n - m + 1$ is 64 and the other is 1. Which can it be?

If $n + m = 1$ it tells us that the sum of the first and the last term is 1. How can that be if you want to have a sum of 32?

On the other hand, if $n - m + 1 = 1$. Since $n - m + 1$ is the number of terms, the number of consecutive numbers, we know that the number of terms is 1. But we said in the original problem that we were looking at positive integers that cannot be written as **two** or more consecutive positive integers. If $n - m + 1 = 1$, then 32 cannot be written as the sum of two or more consecutive integers.

It looks as if we have just shown that 32 is bad.

In exactly the same way we can show that **any** power of 2 is bad. Try it first for 64, say, or even 16. Then show it for **every** power of 2.

I've gone about as far as I think I can go here with flight maps, but I do want to extend the Consecutive Numbers Problem a little further. Recall we said a number was **good** if it can be written as the sum of only **one** string of consecutive numbers. Let's push that idea further. Say that a number is **r-good** if it can be written as the sum of precisely r different strings of consecutive numbers. Note that a good number is 1–good. What can be said about *r*-good numbers in general?

At this point you need to go off and do battle with that idea. When you come back I'll deal with the number 27.

 Going through the usual motions, I'll put

$$27 = \frac{1}{2}(n + m)(n - m + 1).$$

Before I start to solve this, and hopefully to find the *r* for which 27 is *r*-good, I want to look at $n + m$ and $n - m + 1$.

A little while back, on page 169, I showed that if $n + m$ is even, then $n - m + 1$ is odd. Using a similar argument you can prove that, if $n - m + 1$ is even, $n + m$ is odd. So this means that $n + m$ and $n - m + 1$ can't both be even.

But there's more. We showed above that $n - m + 1$ can never be 1. That still holds.

Then finally, before we investigate the number 27, $n + m$ is always bigger than $n - m + 1$. To see this, just subtract $n - m + 1$ from $n + m$.

$$n + m - (n - m + 1) = 2m - 1$$

Now $m \geq 1$ as it is the first term in our string of consecutive numbers. And if $m \geq 1$, $2m - 1 \geq 1 > 0$. So $n + m$ is always bigger than $n - m + 1$.

We are now ready to look at 27.

$$27 = \frac{1}{2}(n + m)(n - m + 1).$$

So $$54 = (n + m)(n - m + 1).$$

And what we need to do now is to find all the factors of 54 and put them equal to $n + m$ or $n - m + 1$. Let's put them down like this:

$n+m$	54^*	27	18	9	$6^\oplus$	$3^\oplus$	$2^\oplus$	$1^\oplus$
$n-m+1$	1	2	3	6	9	18	27	54

Now we know we don't need to look at the numbers marked $*$, where

$$n + m = 54$$

and

$$n - m + 1 = 1$$

simply because $n - m + 1 \neq 1$. And we know that we don't have to look at any of the numbers marked $\oplus$ either, because there

$$n - m + 1 > n + m.$$

So we have three pairs of factors to deal with. I'll do the first one in detail and tell you what happens to the others, but it looks as if 27 might be 3-good.

Case 1 $n + m = 27$ **(1)**
                           $n - m + 1 = 2$ **(2)**

Add **(1)** and **(2)** $2n + 1 = 29$

So $2n = 28$ and then $n = 14$.

If $n = 14$ then, from **(1)**, $m = 13$.

So the string we get here is **13, 14.**

Case 2 $n + m = 18$
                           $n - m + 1 = 3$

This gives $n = 10$, $m = 8$.

So the string here is **8, 9, 10.**

Case 3 $n + m = 9$
                           $n - m + 1 = 6$

So $n = 7$, $m = 2$ and the string is **2, 3, 4, 5, 6, 7.** So 27 is indeed 3-good.

To get stuck into this problem it's worth going back and drawing up another table. Mine below has a cross for bad numbers and the number r for r-good numbers. Do you agree with this table? Can you see any patterns? Does the table go far enough to be of any help?

n	1	2	3	4	5	6	7	8	9	10
r	×	×	1	×	1	1	1	×	2	1
n	11	12	13	14	15	16	17	18	19	20
r	1	1	1	1	3	×	1	2	1	1
n	21	22	23	24	25	26	27	28	29	30
r	3	1	1	1	2	1	3	1	1	3

I think I'd concentrate on the 1-good numbers first. From what I said in the last chapter I'm inclined to think of these in two parts. First, there are clearly the primes. Then it seems to me that there are primes multiplied by powers of 2.

Using the factorisation of $2n$ into $n + m$ and $n - m + 1$, I think I could show that $2^a p$ where a is any non-negative integer and p is any odd prime, has only one string.

What about $r = 2$ though? Here we seem to have only 9, 18 and 25. Are these primes squared? No. 18 isn't a prime squared, but it is of the form $2^a p^2$. Maybe that's what all the 2-good numbers look like.

But there are problems with $r = 3$. The numbers 21 and 27 turn up there. You might like to think that 3-good numbers are just $2^a p^3$ but 21? Do we get $2^a p^3$ and $2^a pq$ for a any non-negative integer and p, q odd primes?

What's your guess for $r = 4$? Or $r = 5$? Or $r = 6$? Or .... Can you prove any of these?

Put n points on the boundary of a circle. What is the largest number of regions into which we can divide the circle by joining the n points with lines?

As with all problems, a bit of experimenting seems to be in order. So we'll draw some small cases and try to understand what is going on.

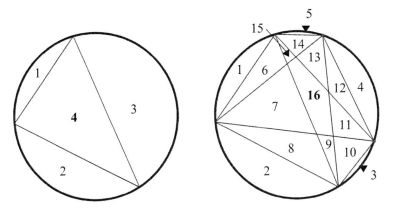

Figure 17.1 Dividing a circle into regions. Two initial cases:
$n = 3$ (4 regions) and $n = 5$ (16 regions).

As the result of the sketches in **Figure 17.1** and various other experiments we get some numbers that can be put into an incomplete (as yet) table. Here, R is the largest number of regions for a given value of n points.

n	1	2	3	4	5	6	7	8	9	10	11	12
R	1	2	4	8	16							

You have to be very careful in both drawing the different situations and counting the number of regions. It's a good idea, especially as the number of regions starts to get large, to put different numbers in each region. Even then, some small regions tend to get omitted. You also have to be careful not to let three lines cross in one point; recall we are trying to find the **largest** number of regions that we can get for each n. It does help to check things as you go. By the time you get to around $n = 8$ and 9, your drawings get a little rubbery and you may get different values of R each time you draw a specific n. You won't necessarily be able to trust your drawings.

But is there any point going past five points on the boundary of the circle? The pattern is surely clear.

 **Conjecture:** $R = 2^{n-1}.$

It seems that putting in each new point will just double the number of regions. So we should be able to find some sort of induction argument to prove that. Isn't it the case that every line from this new point will cut a previous region in two? All we have to do is to formalise this obvious argument.

On the other hand, it may well be worth your while carefully constructing circles when $n = 6,\ 7$ or 8 in the hope of finding a counterexample. This will, of course, save you having to think up a proof, for the moment anyway.

▷ Let's go back to flight maps (Chapters 16 and 17) but take away the restriction that the dots have to be labelled. This means that the objects labelled (a) and (b) in **Figure 17.2**, **graphs** we'll call them, are this time the same. Essentially we can take the vertices in **Figure 17.2** (a) and put them on top of the vertices in **Figure 17.2** (b) so that the lines of **Figure 17.2** (a) lie on top of the lines of **Figure 17.2** (b).

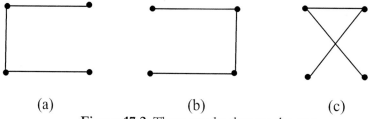

(a)   (b)   (c)

Figure 17.2 Three graphs that are the same.

Actually the same thing can be done to **Figures 17.2** (a) and **17.2** (c). So there are many ways of drawing the graph of **Figure 17.2** (a), but all the graphs are essentially the same: they all have four dots and three lines and the graph has the property that two dots have one line coming out of them and the other dots have two lines coming out of them.

If you experiment for a while you should be able to justify that in **Figure 17.3** below; we have a complete list of all the graphs on one to three dots.

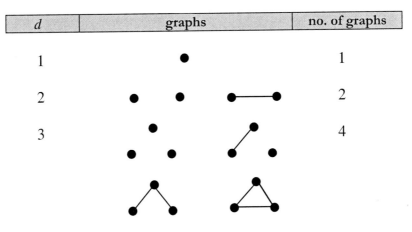

d	graphs	no. of graphs
1		1
2		2
3		4

Figure 17.3 The graphs on up to three dots.

To obtain these results you have to repeat what we did with flight maps and ignore lines that start and finish with the same dot. Also restrict the diagrams so that there is, at most, one line between two dots. You might like to follow this up by checking that there are eight graphs on four vertices. (This is, after all, the obvious conjecture.)

Going back to the Regions Problem you may only have been able to find 31 regions for $n = 6$ or you may have convinced yourself that a Proof by Induction did work. I'd suggest that you check whichever of these you did. Only one can be right.

I've also been working and I've come up with the following table by drawing regions for n up to 9.

n	1	2	3	4	5	6	7	8	9	10	11	12
R	1	2	4	8	16	31	57	99	163			

What is going on here?

I've slipped this problem in just to remind us all that we can't take patterns that turn up in tables for granted. There is no guarantee that a pattern that seems to be working up to a certain value of n will work for all values of n.

Pattern chasing is a good start to the solution of many problems, but **it is only a step along the way.** If the pattern can't be justified you can't be sure that the pattern is the answer that you are after. And to do any such justification, you have to go back to the problem itself.

If you recall the Four Colour Theorem, I think that pretty well everyone believed, long before it was proved, that you didn't need more than four colours to colour any map, and cartographers certainly found this in practice, but mathematicians worked hard for over a 120 years to make sure that they could prove it.

On the other hand, a guessed pattern can turn out not to be a pattern after a certain number of cases. I give an example below of one that happened during some research I was involved in.

I had been working with a group of people on sorting machines. We were looking at streams of numbers, permutations of the numbers 1 through n, that arrive at a machine and the machine tries to sort them. Let's look at a simple case. Suppose the numbers come in and we put them on a pile. We want the numbers to go out of the machine in the correct order so a larger number can't be taken off the pile until every number smaller than it has gone. Suppose that 1324 (in that order) was fed into the machine:

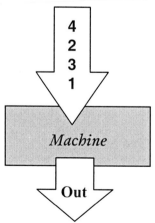

Then 1 would go on the pile, but could immediately be sent out as it is the first number. Then 3 arrives, but 3 can't leave until 2 is sent out. So then 2 comes in and sits on top of 3. Clearly the machine is able to send off 2 and then immediately it can send off 3. Finally 4 comes in and is sent out straight away. This means that our simple sorting machine can sort 1324.

The question that we are asking is, "What can we say about incoming permutations that can't be sorted?" In particular, "Out of all permutations of n objects, how many are not able to be sorted by a given machine?" In our work we came across a machine for which the numbers are as shown in the table. Here P is the number of permutations of n objects that can't be sorted by the machine.

n	1	2	3	4	5	6	7	8	9
P	1	2	4	8	16	32	64	128	256

This has power of two written all over it. The difficulty was, of course, that from the situation we had in front of us we knew that the answer couldn't possibly be a power of two. With the aid of a computer we generated the next set of numbers.

n	10	11	12	13	14	15	16	17	18
P	511	985	1715	2621	3594	4580	5567	6554	7541

If you look closely at these numbers, starting from $n = 10$, you'll see several that are quite weird and seemingly unpredictable. But after a certain stage the difference between successive terms is 987, the sixteenth Fibonacci number! We had certainly found a very interesting pattern. It's not often you get powers of two followed by a mess and then it all straightens out to numbers that have a common difference of the sixteenth Fibonacci number! But how could we be sure that there wasn't another transition period later before some other pattern came into being? So we had to prove that what we thought was happening *was* actually happening. And that turned out to be a little messy but doable. We managed it by using Mathematical Induction to get a recurrence relation and then using generating functions to give a series whose coefficients included these numbers. In fact the numbers that I have reproduced above are just one of an infinite series of related numbers, that are derived from a family of similar sorting machines and they all end up with successive terms differing by a different Fibonacci number.

So, after all that discussion, is the pattern for R a little messy but doable?

Of course there are more than eight graphs on four dots. (You should find 11!) Unfortunately we don't get a nice pattern for the number of graphs on d dots; there's certainly nothing as nice as the number of flight maps. But I want to look further into graphs because we will be able to use them in the next chapter.

One of the things that is important about graphs is the **degree** of a dot. This is just the number of lines that meet at a particular dot. As an example, in **Figure 17.4**, I have put the degree of each dot in a ring next to the dot.

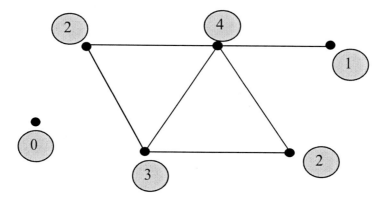

Figure 17.4 A graph with the degrees of its vertices shown

It turns out that almost the first result that you get in graph theory involves degrees. You can discover this relation for yourself by going through all the graphs you've seen so far, along with any that you draw for yourself, and see how degrees and total number of lines are linked. I'll come back to this in the next chapter where I'll find a use for it.

Another result that I'll find useful for graphs is one that the famous Swiss mathematical giant, Euler, discovered. That result is to do with **planar** graphs. These are graphs that you can draw in the plane so that no two lines cross.

The graph in **Figure 17.5** is planar. Clearly, if I were being perverse, I could draw it so that two lines **did** cross, but I'm keen to keep lines **uncrossed** if I possibly can. Just as in **Figure 17.5**(a) I have drawn a graph with a crossing, but in **Figure 17.5**(b) I have drawn the same graph without a crossing. So the graph in **Figure 17.5** is a planar graph.

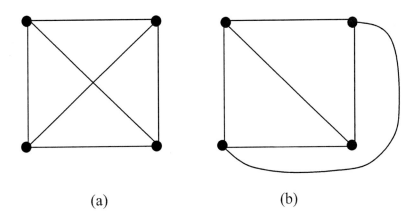

(a)   (b)

Figure 17.5 How a planar graph may look non-planar

For the record, here, in **Figure 17.6**, are a couple of **non-planar** graphs. You might like to see why you can't uncross any of the offending crossed lines.

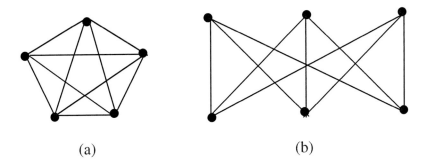

(a)   (b)

Figure 17.6 Two definitely non-planar graphs

Let's be just a little more specific with our planar graphs. I want them to be **connected**. You see I'm very much concerned for amorous ants who live on dots in a graph and would like to get to see each other from time to time. For deep physical reasons, they can only travel from dot to dot by lines of the graph. So in graphs that are not connected they may never be able to get to see each other. The graph in **Figure 17.4** is not connected. This is not the case for the graphs of **Figures 17.5** and **17.6**. They are definitely ant friendly.

And the final idea I want to introduce for planar graphs is the idea of a **face**. This is simply the smallest region of the plane enclosed by lines. The graph in **Figure 17.5** (b) has four faces, while the graph in

Figure 17.4 has only three faces. We have to use the entire plane up when we take the union of all the faces.

So let f be the number of faces in a connected planar graph. Can you find a relation linking d, l and f for **all** such graphs, where l is the number of lines in the graph? Perhaps I should note that, for the graph of **Figure 17.5** (b), $d = 4$, $l = 6$ and $f = 4$. Is that any help?

I'll get back to this in the next chapter.

In the meantime you may not have met the **Handshake Problem:** My wife and I went to a party the other weekend. There were four other couples there. As often happens at such events, you shake hands with some people and you don't shake hands with others. Obviously no one shook hands with their partner nor did they shake hands with anyone more than once. Now I take notice of numbers. On talking around I discovered that everyone had shaken hands with a different number of people. Knowing this, and not how many times they had shaken hands, I was able to deduce how many handshakes my wife was involved in. Can you?

Solve; prove; extend; generalise.

In this chapter I want to resolve the issues that were left open in the previous chapter. So I hope to finish with an expression that I can justify for the number of regions as well as saying more about the Handshake Problem. Along the way I'll need to use the little bit of graph theory that I introduced in the last chapter.

Recall the table that I had produced there linked the number of regions, R, with the number of points around the circle, n.

n	1	2	3	4	5	6	7	8	9	10
R	1	2	4	8	16	31	57	99	163	

Those of you who are familiar with the method of differences might have produced the following table of values, where the entry in each new line is the difference between the two numbers above it.

```
1     2     4     8     16      31      57      99      163
   1     2     4     8     15      26      42      64
      1     2     4     7     11      16      22
         1     2     3     4      5      6
            1     1     1     1     1
```

The fact that the fourth differences are all the same tells us that a fourth degree polynomial will fit the original ten entries. You can work this out by putting down a general quartic equation and successively put in the values of R for the five values of n, other than 1 to 5 (why?). This should get you the following:

$$R = \frac{1}{24}(n^4 - 6n^3 + 23n^2 - 18n + 24).$$

You might like to check my calculations or at least put a few of the values 1 to 9 in the quartic and make sure that they give you the R values in the table.

But the question is "Does this correctly predict the value of R when $n = 10$?" Check that out. Following the previous question quite rapidly comes "Why should a quartic give a better answer than our original power of two expression?" We leave that one for you to think about too.

 The Regions Problem is the archetypical problem given to those people who see no need to justify a pattern that they have just guessed from a table. I talked about this quite a bit in Chapter 14 when I was turning the fishes. There I made a point of the fact that given the numbers

$$1, 2, 3, 5, 8,$$

there are an infinite number of ways to extend that to a 'respectable' sequence all of whose terms fit a well defined rule. Now I am showing you the sequence starter 1, 2, 4, 8, 16 which has some implied rule because it comes from the Regions Problem, but that implied rule is *not* the 'obvious' one, even though the 'obvious' one fits it for fully *five* values of n. That length of compatibility would be enough to convince most people that they had the pattern. However, I'm sorry to say, it doesn't convince a mathematician. (Note that what I have said about 'people' above, also doesn't apply to anyone from Missouri.)

So it is all right for young students to guess a pattern, but even the youngest and most inexperienced should be asked why they think that pattern holds. More insistence on this should be made as the students get older. Certainly they should be gradually convinced that proofs are needed. The older they get, the more opportunity and encouragement they should be given to produce justifications or proofs.

In order to justify my quartic I need to show you some more graph theory.

Two Results from Graph Theory: The first result that is usually introduced into a graph theory class is the link between degrees and lines. It's not a deep result. If you look at the graph in Figure 4 in Chapter 17, you'll see that if you add up the degrees of the dots (vertices), you get 12 and there are 6 lines. Repeating this on the graph of Figure 5 you get 12 for the sum of the degrees and 6 for the lines. Going to Figure 6, the graph in (a) gives you 20 and 10, while the one in (b) gives 18 and 9. It looks as though we have:

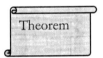

Theorem   The sum of the degrees of all the dots of a graph is twice the number of lines.

Proof   Think of any line between any two dots. This line is counted first in the degree of the first dot and secondly in the degree of the second dot. So every line is counted twice in the sum of the degrees of the dots. That's all!

Now it's the turn of Euler. The following result is usually called **Euler's Polyhedral Formula**.

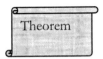

Theorem   If you include in the count f, the face that surrounds all of a connected planar graph, then we have Euler's Polyhedral Formula.

$$d - l + f = 2$$

Proof   I'll prove this in a fudgy sort of way by Induction on d. Which parts are the fudgy ones and need to be fixed to make the proof watertight I'll leave to you to figure out. Try to fix what you don't entirely believe.

Step 1.   If $d = 1$ we have the single graph on one dot that has no lines and the one external face. So $d = 1 = f$ and $l = 0$. Clearly $d - l + f = 2$.

Step 2.   I'm now going to assume that the Formula is true for $d = k$. So any connected planar graph on k dots with l_k lines and f_k faces satisfies the equation

$$k - l_k + f_k = 2.$$

Step 3.   Take any connected planar graph on $k + 1$ dots.

Remove a dot from this graph and also remove all of the lines joining that dot to the rest of the graph. I've shown this schematically in

Figure 1. The shaded blob is the k dot graph that remains after one of the dots u is removed.

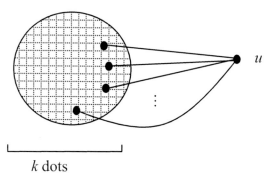

k dots

Figure 18.1 Setting up an induction proof of Euler's Polyhedral Formula

The graph left on removing u has k dots, so it satisfies

$$k - l_k + f_k = 2$$

and I want to show that

$$(k+1) - l_{k+1} + f_{k+1} = 2,$$

where l_{k+1} and f_{k+1} are the number of lines and faces, respectively in my $k+1$ dot graph.

Suppose that u has degree g. Then removing u from the graph removes g lines. This means

$$l_{k+1} = g + l_k.$$

Further, the dot u is surrounded by g faces in the $k+1$ dot graph. All but one of these (the outside face) is destroyed when u is removed. So

$$f_{k+1} = f_k + (g - 1).$$

Let's do some accounting.

$$(k+1) - l_{k+1} + f_{k+1} = (k+1) - (g + l_k) + (f_k + g - 1)$$
$$= k + 1 - g - l_k + f_k + g - 1$$
$$= k - l_k + f_k$$

But by Step 2 we know this is 2. So we've proved what we set out to prove.

So what didn't you like about this proof? A couple of things occur to me but I don't guarantee that I've found all the problems that you have. For instance, in the Induction proof I really should have justified the fact that there is a dot u in the $k+1$ dot graph, whose removal gives me a **connected,** planar, graph. This is because I need those conditions for the equation in Step 2 to hold. Remember that the graphs I'm working with have to be **connected** and **planar**. So I need to show that the k dot graph has both of those conditions. The planarity is easy. How could removing a dot and some lines suddenly force two lines to cross? If they were crossed after I removed u they were crossed before. So we need to make sure that removing u doesn't lead to a disconnected graph on k dots.

Now I'm sorry, but I'm going to duck the connectedness. It can be justified by a spanning tree argument, but I'd rather not go there right now. Can I suggest you try the web? You might also get hold of Lakatos' book, *Proof and Refutations*, to see how purported proofs, like this one, can be poo-pooed. The book by Imre Lakatos, *Proofs and Refutations (The Logic of Mathemtical Discovery)* Cambridge University Press, 1976, is well worth delving into as you struggle with the idea of solving problems. As one web reviewer, Stavros Macrakis, says "In this brilliant and deep -- yet easy to read -- book, Lakatos shows how mathematicians explore concepts; how their ideas can develop over time; and how misleading the "textbook" presentation of math really is."

There is a hint that the Handshake Problem may be solved using Graph Theory since the Problem was introduced in the chapter that Graph Theory first made an appearance. Suppose you draw up a graph with a dot for each person, ten dots in all, and then for any two people who shook hands we join the dots representing them. The number of handshakes each person made is the degree of their dot. Now it will certainly help if you draw diagrams as I move through the argument.

Since there are only nine other people who can shake hands with any individual the degrees of the ten points could be any of the numbers 0, 1, 2, 3, 4, 5, 6, 7, 8, 9. But if someone shook 9 hands, then that person would have shaken **everyone** else's hand and then no one could have degree 0.

Fine. So for the nine people other than me **either** they had shaken hands 0, 1, 2, 3, 4, 5, 6, 7, 8 times and I had shaken hands some number of times (other than 9) **or** they had shaken hands 1, 2, 3, 4, 5, 6, 7, 8, 9 times and I had shaken hands some number of times.

But again, if someone had shaken hands nine times they would have had to have shaken hands with their partner – and this is not to be the case. Therefore no one had shaken hands 9 times. So someone must have shaken hands eight times.

Think about the person who shook hands eight times. They must surely be the partner of the person with the degree of 0 (because everyone else has a non-zero degree). Let's remove these two from our graph. As this removes the degree 0 person and the degree 8 person, the remaining degrees are all reduced by 1 to give 0, 1, 2, 3, 4, 5, 6 (and of course, there's still me).

At this point the argument cascades. The 0 and 6 are partners, so remove them, This leaves 0, 1, 2, 3, 4 (and me). But 0 and 4 are partners. On their removal we get 0, 1, 2 (and me)., Remove good old 0 and 2 to get 0 (and me).

The final 0 must be **my** partner. And she shook hands with the person who was originally degree 8; the reduced first step person of degree 6; the reduced second step person of degree 4; and the reduced final step person of degree 2. My wife shook four hands. But what about me?

 Let me now try to sew up the original Regions Problem and show that

$$R = \frac{1}{24}(n^4 - 6n^3 + 23n^2 - 18n + 24).$$

is exactly where we want to be. What's more let's also see that that horrible quartic really arises naturally. And the person who deserves the praise for this is Timothy Murphy — see '*The dissection of a circle by chords!*' that appeared in the Mathematical Gazette in May 1972, pages 113-115.

I'm going to go the long way round here and first show how the proof works for the particular case of $n = 5$.

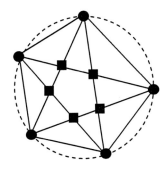

Figure 18.2 The Regions Problem for $n = 5$

First note that in **Figure 18.2**, I've drawn the given circle as a dotted line. Further, I'll draw each one of the original points on the given circle as a filled-in circle and I'll call them **circular points**. The chords joining circular points together intersect at points in the interior of the dotted circle. These points will be drawn as a filled-in square and, therefore, referred to as **square points**.

I now want to think of the solid part of the diagram in **Figure 18.2**, the part not containing the dotted line, as a graph.

We know that there are five circular points because we are dealing with the case $n = 5$. But how do we know that there are five 'square' points? When you think about it, each one of these square dots is at the intersection of two of the original chords. And for every choice of the original four points on the circle, we get one square point. Just check that out. Now I'll call this number of choices $^5C_4$ (which we know is 5). In the general case with n original points, each one of the corresponding square points arises after a choice of four of the original points and I'll write this as $^nC_4$.

Going back to the solid graph of **Figure 18.2**, I now have five original points as dots and $^5C_4$ square dots. If I want to count faces, perhaps I can use Euler's Polyhedral Formula because I know d and with a bit of luck I can find l.

Think about l. From our degree-lines link we know that

$$2l = \text{sum of the degrees of the solid graph.}$$

Now the degrees of the circular points are 4 because each of the original points is joined to four others. Also the degrees of the square points are 4 because they are formed by the crossing of two of the original lines.

So $$2l = 5 \times 4 + {}^5C_4 \times 4 = 5 \times 4 + 5 \times 4 = 40.$$

That means that $l = 20$. By Euler

$$d - l + f = 2,$$

So $$f = 2 - d + l$$
$$= 2 - 10 + 20 = 12.$$

When you think about it, one of these faces is **outside** the solid graph, which means it's not one of the regions we're trying to count. But we do now have tags on 11 of the required regions. And the other regions are formed by the dotted links between the circular points and the solid links between the circular points. There are five of these. Hence we have the $11 + 5 = 16$ regions that we wanted.

Have another look over that, then take a deep breath and follow me on the general argument.

Fine, so we need to find f, the number of faces for the equivalent of the solid graph in the n point case. Then we subtract 1 to release the outside face. There are then $f - 1$ regions enclosed by the solid graph.

The other regions are again enclosed between the dotted lines joining the original points and the solid lines between those points. There are n of these. Our final count then is $R = f - 1 + n$. It's now only a matter of finding f and we're done.

It's all down to Euler. First $d = n + {}^nC_4$. This is just the circular points plus the square points.

How about l? Since $2l = $ sum of degrees, we need to find the degrees. Each of the n circular points is joined to $n - 1$ other original points by straight lines (before we introduce the square points). So we have n points of degree $n - 1$. As for the square points, there are ${}^nC_4$ of them and each has degree 4. So

$$2l = n(n-1) + 4 \,{}^nC_4.$$

This gives $l = \dfrac{n(n-1)}{2} + 2\,{}^nC_4$

Going back to Euler, we see

$$f = 2 - d + l$$
$$= 2 - (n + {}^nC_4) + \frac{n(n-1)}{2} + 2\,{}^nC_4.$$

The big one that we want is R. And

$$R = f - 1 + n$$
$$= \left[2 - (n + {}^nC_4 + \frac{n(n-1)}{2} + 2\,{}^nC_4\right] - 1 + n$$
$$= 1 + \frac{n(n-1)}{2} + {}^nC_4.$$

It all depends on ${}^nC_4$. What is this? Well, ${}^nC_4$ is just the number of ways of choosing four things from n things. If we were thinking of doing this from scratch $\cdots$ well, let's do ${}^nC_2$ first.

${}^nC_2$ is the number of ways of choosing two things from n things. If we were thinking of doing this from scratch, we might choose the first one in n ways and that would mean that we would have $n-1$ choices for the second one. At first sight that gives us $n(n-1)$. However, if you check this out for $n = 3$, say, you see that we are out by a factor of 2. This is because any two things can be chosen in two ways. Hence

$$ {}^nC_2 = \frac{1}{2}n(n-1).$$

Hmmm! That's interesting,

$$R = 1 + {}^nC_2 + {}^nC_4!$$

But let's go on to ${}^nC_3$. Again the naïve way to count the number of choices of three things from n is to choose n of them first, then

$n - 1$ of them next, and finally $n - 2$ of them. This makes it look like $n(n - 1)(n - 2)$ until you realise that we have over- counted by a factor of 6. So

$$^{n}C_3 = \frac{1}{6} n(n - 1)(n - 2).$$

In the same way,

$$^{n}C_4 = \frac{1}{24} n(n - 1)(n - 2)(n - 3).$$

You can see about now, where that strange factor of 24 might be coming from in the expression

$$\frac{1}{24}(n^4 - 6n^3 + 23n^2 - 18n + 24).$$

I could do the algebra for you but it's not too hard to show that

$$1 + \frac{n(n-1)}{2} + \frac{1}{24} n(n - 1)(n - 2)(n - 3)$$
$$= \frac{1}{24}(n^4 - 6n^3 + 23n^2 - 18n + 24).$$

 Here is another look at the Handshake Problem with a complete proof.

There are 9 people who could shake hands with any individual but one of the nine is that individual's spouse. Since we are told that no person shakes hands with their spouse then the only possible values for the number of handshakes for the 9 visitors apart from myself are 0, 1, 2, 3, 4, 5, 6, 7 and 8. We are told these 9 people have different numbers for the number of hands shaken so there must be one person associated with each of these numbers.

Suppose A shakes 8 hands, B shakes 7 hands, C shakes 6 hands, . . . , H shakes 1 hand and I shakes no hands. Representing A, B, . . . , I by dots, we will join two dots if the corresponding couple shake hands.

There is one extra feature and that is 'ME'. The number of hands I shake cannot be 9 since I don't shake hands with my wife and must, therefore, be the same as one of the individuals A, B, . . . , I. We don't yet know which. I'll include a dot for ME as well. Thus we have:

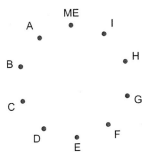

Consider the lines from A. There must be 8 of them. No line can be joined to I, since I doesn't shake hands with anyone. Also A does not shake hands with A so the 8 people left must be joined to A. Therefore we can draw some of the lines of the graph:

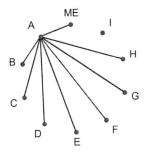

Since I is the only person that doesn't shake hands with A, then A and I are a married couple.

Next, consider B who shakes 7 hands. One of these is A, leaving 6 others. But I shakes hands with nobody and H, who shakes only one hand, shakes hands with A. So these two are ruled out of shaking hands with B and so the 6 others are C, D, E, F, G and ME. The graph now looks like:

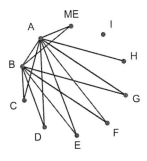

B doesn't shake hands with I or H so, since I is already accounted for, B and H must be a married couple.

Next, C already shakes hands with B and A, cannot shake hands with I, H and now G. The remaining four (D, E, F and ME), together with A and B must be the 6 who shake hands with C. The graph becomes:

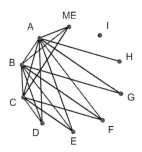

Using a similar argument, C and G are a married couple.

D only requires two more people to shake hands with and, since now F has the required quota, they must be E and ME, making the graph:

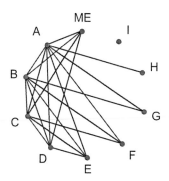

D and F are a married couple leaving E as my wife. The graph is finished since everyone shakes hands with the required number of guests.

From the graph you can see that:

- my wife shakes hands with 4 people;
- while I shake hands with the same 4.

But you knew that anyway – didn't you ?

19 *Problem Solving in the Curriculum*

Although most of the problems in this book require some knowledge from the school curriculum, they largely stand apart from it. In this chapter I want to present some problems that are placed directly in the secondary school curriculum. The first of these are to do with basic geometry. The next is a way to introduce a well known generalisation of Pythagoras' Theorem and the last is an investigation involving calculus. I've put these problems here to show that problem solving **can** be used in school mathematics and, I think, **should** be used.

I have not included here the proof of the formula for the sum of an Arithmetic Progression, but it is essentially done in Chapter 15. If you start with formally finding the sum of the numbers from 1 to 100, the same approach will get you any sum of consecutive numbers, then any specific arithmetic progression, and finally the sum of the general arithmetic progression. I leave the details to you.

I should also note first that I have some personal experiences to show that a problem solving approach can work in schools. These are both from research that I was involved in. The first was in a primary school. There the teacher was surprised that she managed to cover the curriculum more quickly using a problem solving approach. She said that initially it took time so she was behind her normal progress after the first term. However, once the children got the idea, then they picked up new ideas more quickly than her students had done in previous years. Overall then she thought that her students went a little faster and understood more.

The other piece of research was in a secondary school with a weaker class. These students had one problem solving lesson a week. No one noticed much obvious progress until the exam at the end of the year. Then they did much better than the corresponding class had done in previous years. Furthermore some of the students did better than students in supposedly better classes.

So it is worth trying at least some problem solving during the year. The problem that may worry you is that you have to be prepared for anything. You never know quite what students will come up with. So there is a potential challenge there, but it could make teaching more exciting and interesting for you.

 I want to first look at two elementary results: the sum of the angles of a triangle is 180° and the area of a triangle is a half of the base times the height.

I think that many teachers get students to cut out a triangle and then urge them to tear off the angles. The angles can be reassembled to make what appears to be a straight line. This can easily become a more developed problem solving exercise by asking the students to cut out a triangle and then ask them what the sum of the angles is. Someone might say "Measure them all and add them up". This is worth doing, so let some of the class do that. Then ask if they can think of another way and lead them to the edge tearing method.

But how can they prove that the conjecture they have now have about 180° ? Get them to take a fresh triangle and only tear off *two* of the angles. Now in how many ways can they put the torn angles together with the untorn angle? There are six possible diagrams that they might get but I will restrict myself to looking at one of the following two. In the other four possibilities it's also important to move the class to the parallel idea in order to get a proof.

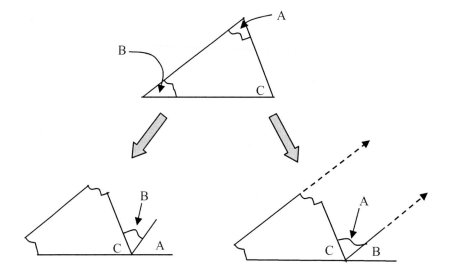

Figure 19.1 Two ways of re-assembling the angles of a triangle

Is any one of these **nicer** than the other? Get them to see that the second diagram has a 'line' parallel to one of the sides of the original triangle. This should lead to the use of the properties of parallel lines to show that the angles add to 180°.

Starting with a triangle it should be easy to lead the students to seeing that there is a parallelogram with twice its area - just put two copies of one triangle next to each other along a side. So we now have the problem of showing that the parallelogram has the same area as a rectangle. This shouldn't be too hard using paper again and cutting out the appropriate triangle (along the dotted line on the left of **Figure 19.2**) from the parallelogram.

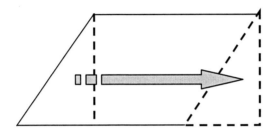

Figure 19.2 A parallelogram and a rectangle with equal areas.

But does this work for **all** parallelograms? How about this one (**Figure 19.3**)?

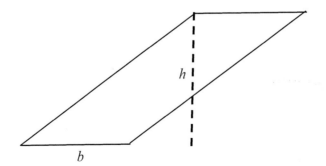

Figure 19.3 A 'difficult' parallelogram

The problem here is that the perpendicular from the corresponding point lands outside the base - whose length is b. So the simple cut and replace method for the triangle in **Figure 19.2** doesn't work! How can we get around this? Someone is sure to say "*Place the parallelogram on its left side*"! But that doesn't give us $b \times h$. We now can't be sure that the area of a parallelogram is **any** base by the corresponding height. It is possible to do this by 'cutting' but it takes a little more effort. And then have all cases been covered? (I'd like to thank Kaye Stacey and Helen Chick for introducing me to the problem with the area of a parallelogram.)

 Think about Pythagoras' Theorem. How can we generalise or extend it?

I suppose that the most famous generalisation of Pythagoras' Theorem in recent times was proved by Andrew Wiles in 1995 (with a little help from his friends) after it had been sitting around, sneering at all attempts to show its truth or falsehood since about 1630 when Fermat first scribbled it in the margin of his book.

Actually Wiles did a relatively unusual thing while proving Fermat's Last Theorem – he shut himself away and worked on the problem in virtual mathematical isolation. In much the same way as the fictional Uncle Petros did when trying to solve Goldbach's Conjecture – see *Uncle Petros and Goldbach's Conjecture* by Apostolos Doxiadis, published by Faber and Faber in 2000. Actually, what I say now is too late for you, but the publishers offered a prize of one million dollars if anyone could prove Goldbach's Conjecture within two years of publication.

Goldbach's Conjecture, made in 1742, is that every even number bigger than 2 is the sum of two prime numbers. We know that the Conjecture is true for any even number up to about 10^{18}.

The book is reviewed on line by Keith Devlin who says "Indeed, through the medium of a fictional story, he (the author) manages to convey the nature of pure mathematics, the passion that can drive a mathematician to work for years on a seemingly irrelevant problem, and the single-minded dedication it can take to see the project through to its end -- or not, as the case may be."

But shutting yourself away to do mathematics isn't quite as rare as I would have thought these days. Grigory Perelman used this approach while he proved Poincaré's Conjecture (2006). (I recommend that you look Perelman up on the web. His story makes interesting reading.)

Both Wiles and Perelman had their work subject to great scrutiny before their proofs were accepted. It was during this process that an error was found in Wiles' original work. However, with the help of a colleague called Taylor, he was able to find a way round the problem. Now this checking of both Perelman's and Wiles' work is not unusual. When any mathematician proves a result they generally want to have it published in one of the mathematical journals. This way it establishes that it is theirs, it has developed mathematics further, and it counts towards their promotion. But every such publication is refereed to make sure that (i) it is correct and (ii) it is of relevance to the journal's readership.

Now in the 17th century, Fermat had obviously been inspired by Pythagorean triples to look at the situation of

$$x^n + y^n = z^n, \text{ for } n > 2.$$

It is well-known that for $n = 2$, the last equation has integer solutions for x, y and z (the Pythagorean triples), but Fermat claimed to be able to show that there were no such solutions for $n > 2$. However, he also claimed that the margin was too small for him to put down a proof! Fermat doesn't in fact seem to have had a proof, but he did manage to prove it for $n = 4$ and may have had a proof for $n = 3$ as well.

Anyway, the problem aroused attention. Gradually different mathematicians were able to produce proofs for different values of n. When computers became more readily available it became possible to produce exhaustive proofs for n a prime up to quite large sizes. (It soon became clear that it was sufficient to prove the result for n a prime.) Until Wiles came along, what became known as Fermat's Last Theorem (even though it wasn't yet a theorem but only a conjecture) stuttered along with specific cases being proved much the way the 400 Problem or one of our other problems did.

But this wasn't the generalisation that I was thinking about. Nor is it the one that was found by Hoehn and is included in Pritchard's book *The Changing Shape of Geometry: Celebrating a Century of Geometry and Geometry Teaching* (CUP/MAA Spectrum, 2003). The one I'm thinking about is part of the school curriculum and I wanted to talk about it simply because I think that it is important that regular curriculum material be presented as problems for students to try to solve.

For other generalisations see

www.cut-the-knot.org/pythagoras/index.shtml.

Here is the problem. Pythagoras' Theorem says that for a right angled triangle,

$$h^2 = a^2 + b^2 ,$$

where h is the hypotenuse and a and b are the lengths of the other two sides. But is there a similar result, a generalisation even, for non-right angled triangles? And if there were, how would we discover it?

Well, we have become used to experimenting to see what happens in new situations. Why not experiment here? Simply set up a whole collection of triangles, measure their sides and see if there is a link between the sides that we might be able to prove.

That sounds fine until you think about it a bit, so it would be a good idea to have a class discussion first. How are you going to do the measuring and how will you handle the data at the end to see what the pattern is? To answer the first question you might just get the whole class at work with their rulers and protractors and knock off 20 or so triangles each. This can be made a lot more efficient by using *Geometer's Sketchpad* or some other technological tool. But before you get under way it might be worth thinking about the end game so that you make it easier for yourselves to handle the large quantity of data that you might produce.

It's likely that there are three independent variables to deal with. These are probably going to be two sides of the triangle and the included angle. To get some idea how each of these contributes to the length of the third side it might be worth planning ahead and keeping the lengths of the two sides fixed while we vary the angle between them. So why not first put the two sides equal to 1 and vary the angle from 10° to 20° to 30° to 40° to …?

As far as the data goes you should discuss these with the class too. How far off Pythagoras' Theorem is the more general situation likely to be? It might be useful to see how far from the Theorem your results are. So if we start out with sides of length 1, by how much do your measurements differ from $\sqrt{2}$? As each new triangle's 'opposite' side is determined, the difference between it and $\sqrt{2}$ can be put on a graph and you can get some idea of what's going on. It is rather comforting to see that there is clearly a pronounced oscillation that suggests a trigonometric function is involved.

Having got this far how are you to proceed? Ask the students what needs to be done next. It looks as if you are on the right track, but how will you find the amplitude of the trigonometric function? Perhaps this is best to be taken a step at a time. Keep one of the independent sides at 1 and change the other before varying the angle again.

This should lead them to conjecture the Cosine Rule. But how is this proved?

In the diagram let AD be the perpendicular from A to D, $AC = b$, $BC = a$, $AB = c$ and angle $ACB = C$.

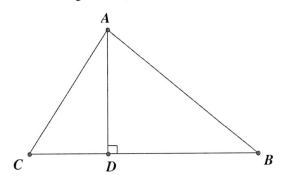

Figure 19.4 Proving the Cosine Rule

Then $AD = b \sin C$ and $CD = b \cos C$. This means that

$$BD = BC - CD = a - b \cos C.$$

We can now apply Pythagoras' Theorem to triangle ABD. Then we find that
$$c^2 = (b \sin C)^2 + (a - b \cos C)^2.$$

And since $\sin^2 C + \cos^2 C = 1$, this tidies up nicely to give

$$c^2 = a^2 + b^2 - 2bc \cos C,$$

the generalisation of Pythagoras' Theorem that is the Cosine Rule.

Of course, philosophically speaking, we have a couple of problems here. First of all the way the diagram has been set up we really have only covered the case where C is less than 90°. This is not such a problem as we can draw the diagram to suit C greater than 90° (see **Figure 19.5**) and things will work out in much the same way as they did above using some basic trigonometry.

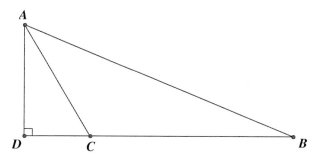

Figure 19.5 The Cosine Rule for C bigger than 90°.

The second problem is that we have used Pythagoras' Theorem to prove the Cosine Rule. This means that we have a different situation here to the Six Circle Problem and the 400 Problem that we have tackled in earlier chapters. There we were able to prove the general results that we got and found that the specific cases that we started from came out as a special case. There's no way that we can say here that Pythagoras' Theorem follows as a special case from our proof of the Cosine Rule – it clearly doesn't as we relied on Pythagoras' Theorem in the proof. But proofs of the Cosine Rule do exist that don't use Pythagoras (if you don't know of one you might look it up on the web). So this independence isn't really a problem.

▷ Now, to change tack, somewhere along the line, everything that is in the school mathematics curriculum must have been discovered and then proved. That means that there are likely to be some things in what we teach that the students can reconstruct. But does this have any benefits? Certainly! For example there is a good chance that students will remember something better if they have worked on it like this – somehow they will know it more intimately because they were involved. And then, if at some later time they have forgotten it, maybe they will remember how to reconstruct it. This might help to give students more control over the subject and see how to 'invent' something else further down the line. But perhaps most of all, it is important for them to see mathematics as a growing subject and to see how some parts of the subject grow and how someone before them did the growing. Hopefully this sort of activity demystifies the subject somewhat.

While we're being philosophical, it's worth recalling that Pythagoras lived to about the age of a 100, not a bad life span for that time. However, a Babylonian fragment from about 1000 BC (500 years before Pythagoras) shows a demonstration of Pythagoras' Theorem for a hypotenuse of $\sqrt{2}$. It is more than likely that the Chinese and the Indians both knew about the result long before Pythagoras. So is it time to stop calling it Pythagoras' Theorem?

And maybe it's worth mentioning here why neither Perelman nor Wiles will get a Nobel Prize for their outstanding work. It's simply because there is **no** Nobel Prize for mathematics. I won't go into the scurrilous rumours, but you might like to look up

http://almaz.com/nobel/why_no_math.html#story

Mathematics has its own prize the **Fields Medal**. But then I have to say why Perelman was awarded a Fields Medal and Wiles wasn't – it is all a matter of age, 40 years in fact. The Medal is only given to mathematicians under 40. When he completed his work on Fermat's Last Theorem, Wiles was over 40. But it doesn't finish there. Perelman didn't accept the Medal! You might look this up on the web too. And you may be even more surprised that Perelman didn't accept a million dollar prize that had been especially created for anyone who solved another long standing and important problem, the Poincaré Conjecture!

▷ My next problem came from a professional development session that Anthony Harradine gave on CAS calculators, so here is another problem that is much more accessible now that CAS calculators exist. (Actually, a graphics calculator will get you a long way here.) Anthony led up to it by some examples such as the ones I'll introduce in a moment. But in his session he didn't have time to extend or generalise the problem, as I do later.

So first of all sketch
$$y = x^2 - 2x + 4.$$

You can make a reasonable free-hand sketch if you like but a computer drawing will be more accurate and might be more useful.

Fine, now sketch

$$y = -2x^2 + 4x + 1.$$

What do these two graphs have in common? What else do both of these graphs have in common?

Is there another quadratic graph that has the same properties as the original two graphs?

The original two questions may have been a little obtuse. What I was thinking of here is that both graphs pass through the point $(1, 4)$ and have zero gradient there. With a little work you can see that $y = 2x^2 - 4x + 5$ also has these properties.

About now I have to ask "How many quadratics have these two properties?" Hopefully this will lead to a discussion of infinity and the introduction of the idea of parameters in the production of

$$y = ax^2 - 2ax + (a + 3).$$

But this can lead to at least three generalisations. First, you might ask how any quadratics can be made to be part of this infinite family. Second, you might ask if there are cubics or other polynomials (or other functions) with the same two basic features that the original two graphs have in common. Third, you might look for some other basic features that you might want quadratics to have, starting with them all passing through a given point where they all have the same gradient. And fourth, so I can't count (I did say 'at least'), extend the idea to cubics again. In this case you might want to have three basic properties, say common point with common gradient with the common point being a point of inflexion. Perhaps you can even go further than that.

In the process of doing all of this, students will have the opportunity to practice basic algebra and calculus skills while at the same time having the opportunity to think like a mathematician. And this is really what this whole book is about.

Appendix I The Problems

The 400 Problem (Chapter 1, page11). You have these two subtractions:

$$
\begin{array}{r}
4 \quad 0 \quad 0 \\
- \quad a \quad b \quad 4 \\
\hline
. \quad . \quad .
\end{array}
\qquad
\begin{array}{r}
4 \quad a \quad b \\
- \quad 4 \quad 0 \quad 0 \\
\hline
. \quad . \quad .
\end{array}
$$

If the answers are the same for both subtractions, what are the values of a and b?

The Difference Problem (Chapter 2, page 20). Take a two-digit number ab. Reverse the order of the digits to get ba. Subtract the smaller of these from the larger. Repeat with the result and keep going until you find something interesting. How's that for an ill-defined problem?

A 1089 Problem (Chapter 2, page 21). If I take any three-digit number abc; reverse its digits to get cba; subtract the smaller from the larger to get pqr; reverse its digits to get rqp; and add pqr to rqp, will I always get 1089? And if I do, why do I?

Kaprekar's Problem (Chapter 2, page 31). Take any 4-digit number whose digits are not all the same. Now put the digits in descending order. Next reverse the digits. Now subtract the smaller from the larger. Repeat the same process with the resulting number. Keep going. What happens eventually?

The Six Circle Problem (Chapter 4, page 39).

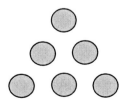

Is it possible to put the numbers 1, 2, 3, 4, 5, 6, one per circle, so that the three numbers on each side of the equilateral triangle have the same sum? If so, how many ways can this be done? If not, why not? Extend or generalise.

The 21 Game (Chapter 7, page 75). There are 21 cubes on the table. Alice and Blair alternatively remove one or two cubes. The winner is the one who takes the last cube.

On the principle of 'ladies first', Alice always takes the first turn. Does Alice have a winning strategy? Does Blair have a winning strategy? Or is it all a matter of luck?

Nim (Chapter 7, page 78). Blocks are placed arbitrarily in two or more piles. When it's their turn Alice and Blair can take any number (at least one) of blocks they like provided they all come from one pile. The winner is the person who takes the last block.

The Frogs Problem (Chapter 9, page 93). Suppose that we have three boy frogs sitting on three lily pads and three girl frogs sitting on another three lily pads. In all there are seven lily pads all in a row with the boy frogs and girl frogs at either end and a spare lily pad in the middle. Frogs can move by sliding to an adjacent empty lily pad or by jumping over one other frog to an empty lily pad. The boy frogs must always keep moving to the end where the girl frogs started and vice versa. Can the boys end up in the girls' original positions and the girls end up in the boys' original positions? If so, what is the smallest number of moves that it takes? If not, why not?

Generalise, extend, and justify everything.

The Rolling Square Problem (Chapter 11, page 117).

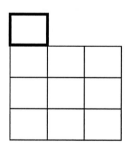

Take a 3 x 3 square and a 1 x 1 square. Put the smaller square, marked in darker lines in the diagram, on the larger one as shown. Now 'roll' the smaller square around the larger one so that it is always in touch with the larger square. What is the locus of any one of the vertices of the smaller square as it rolls around the larger square? In other words, what is the path drawn out by one of the corners?

Extend and generalise.

The Fish Problem (Chapter 13, page 133). The six coins in the diagram on the left, make up a 'fish' facing to the right. What is the smallest number of coins that need to be moved, so that the 'fish' points in the other direction (as on the right)?

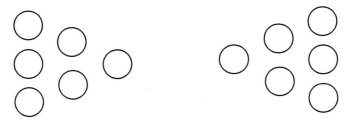

The relative vertical and horizontal positions of the two fish above are irrelevant. The only point here is that the original fish is pointing to the right while the final fish is pointing to the left. It may be that the final fish has been displaced vertically a little.

Generalise, extend, conjecture and prove as much as you can.

The Chessboard Problem (Chapter 13, page 133).

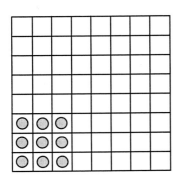

Nine coins are placed on the nine squares in a 3×3 corner of an 8×8 chessboard, see the diagram below. A coin can move **only** by jumping over a neighbouring coin onto an empty chessboard square. This jumping can be horizontal, vertical or diagonal in direction. So, for a start, none of the four corner coins can move. But the centre coin has three possible moves: vertically up; diagonally up and horizontally across.

Using only the moves defined, can the group of nine coins be moved to the 3×3 sub-square in the top right hand corner or the 3×3 sub-square in the bottom right hand corner.

The Consecutive Numbers Problem (Chapter 15, page 155).
Note that $9 = 2 + 3 + 4 = 4 + 5$. In other words, 9 can be written as the sum of consecutive positive integers in two ways. What positive integers *cannot* be written as the sum of two or more consecutive positive integers?

The Flight Map Problem (Chapter 15, page 156). Air New Britain flies to 253 destinations. In its flight magazine there is a map showing these destinations. In the flight map a line joins any two destinations that are linked by an ANB flight. How many different maps are possible? (Allow even the absurd map where none of the 253 destinations is linked by a flight.)

Extend, generalise and prove.

The Regions Problem (Chapter 17, page 173). Put n points on the boundary of a circle. What is the largest number of regions into which we can divide the circle by joining the n points by lines?

The Handshake Problem (Chapter 17, page 180). My wife and I went to a party the other weekend. There were four other couples there. As often happens at such events, you shake hands with some people and you don't shake hands with others. Obviously no one shook hands with their partner nor did they shake hands with anyone more than once. Now I take notice of numbers. On talking around I discovered that everyone had shaken hands with a different number of people. Knowing this, and not how many times they had shaken hands, I was able to deduce how many handshakes my wife was involved in. Can you?

Solve; prove; extend; generalise.

Appendix II Staging Points

Note here that I haven't included all possible staging points. For example, in all problems it is implied that if a conjecture turns out to be false, the students will go back to experimenting and looking for another conjecture.

It is also worth noting that you may decide that it is more valuable for your students to go on to various extensions rather than holding them at a proof point. However, they should know that proofs do exist. In some cases, such as The Frogs Problem, showing them a proof at one stage (with f frogs) may enable them to prove the conjecture at the next stage (with b and g frogs).

The 400 Problem (Chapter 1, page11).

1. Finding a and b in the 400 Problem
2. Generalising to the n00 Problem
3. Proving the n00 Problem
4. Extending to the 4000 Problem
5. Proving it is impossible
6. Finding a, b and c in the 40000 Problem
7. Conjecturing the result for the general problem
8. (a) Understanding a proof of the conjecture
   (b) Proving the conjecture

The Difference Problem (Chapter 2, page 20).

1. Conjecture what is happening for the two-digit case
2. (a) Understanding a proof of the conjecture
   (b) Proving the conjecture
3. Conjecture what is happening for the three-digit case
4. (a) Understanding a proof of the conjecture
   (b) Proving the conjecture
5. Conjecture what is happening for the four-digit case
6. (a) Understanding a proof of the conjecture
   (b) Proving the conjecture
7. Conjecture what is happening for the n-digit case
8. (a) Understanding a proof of the conjecture
   (b) Proving the conjecture

A 1089 Problem (Chapter 2, page 21).

  1. Doing several examples that reach 1089
  2. Noting that palindromes won't produce 1089
  3. (a) Understanding a proof of the conjecture
      (b) Proving the conjecture

The Six Circle Problem (Chapter 4, page 39).

  1. Experimenting
  2. Conjecturing that there are only four answers
  3. (a) Understanding a proof of the conjecture
      (b) Proving the conjecture
  4. Extending the problem in any way
  5. Conjecturing what might happen
  6. (a) Understanding a proof of the conjecture
      (b) Proving the conjecture
  7. Generalising any extension
  8. (a) Understanding a proof of the conjecture
      (b) Proving the conjecture

The 21 Game (Chapter 7, page 75).

  1. Understanding optimum strategies
  2. Knowing how to always win this game
  3. Conjecturing who will win in the n Game
  4. (a) Understanding a proof of the conjecture
      (b) Proving the conjecture
  5. Extending the problem
  6. Making an appropriate conjecture
  7. (a) Understanding a proof of the conjecture
      (b) Proving the conjecture
  8. Generalising or extending further (perhaps to the misère version or more than one pile)
  9. Making a conjecture
  10. (a) Understanding a proof of the conjecture
      (b) Proving the conjecture

Nim (Chapter 7, page 78).

  1. Experimenting
  2. Making a conjecture for the two-pile game
  3. (a) Understanding a proof of the conjecture
      (b) Proving the conjecture